WHO CAN BE AGAINST US?
LEADERSHIP LESSONS FROM
THE LIFE OF PAUL

EDDIE ESTEP

THE FOUNDRY
PUBLISHING®

Cover Design: Bruce Nuffer
Interior Design: Sharon Page

Library of Congress Cataloging-in-Publication Data
A complete catalog record for this book is available from the Library of Congress.

The Internet addresses, email addresses, and phone numbers in this book are ac-
curate at the time of publication. They are provided as a resource. The Foundry
Publishing does not endorse them or vouch for their content or permanence.

10 9 8 7 6 5 4 3 2 1

For my granddaughters, Ellie Kay and Emery Anne,
in hopes that one day they might each be called, like Paul,
"a ringleader of the Nazarene sect" (Acts 24:5).

CONTENTS

Acknowledgments   7
Introduction: The C's of Leadership   9

Part 1: The Leader's Call   13

1. Child of Tarsus: Prelude to Leadership   15
2. Child of Jerusalem: Education   23
3. Child of Damascus: Transformation   32
4. Child of Arabia: Preparation   41
5. Child of Antioch: Ordination   49

Part 2: The Leader's Connections   59

6. First-Circle Connections: Traveling Companions   61
7. Second-Circle Connections: Ministry Colleagues   71
8. Third-Circle Connections: Providential Contacts   81

Part 3: The Leader's Character   89

9. Trustworthy   91
10. Resilient   98
11. Compassionate   107
12. Self-Controlled   115
13. Humble   122

Part 4: The Leader's Competence   131

14. Missional   133
15. Visionary   139
16. Strategic   147
17. Team-Building   161
18. Decisive   170
19. Communicative   176

Part 5: The Leader's Challenges   187

20. Criticism   189
21. Conflict   195
22. Crisis   204

Afterword: The Christlike Leader   215
Notes   217

ACKNOWLEDGMENTS

Special thanks to Diane Estep, Tabita Gonzalez, and Wayne Nelson—the first readers of each chapter's draft—whose input provided helpful direction on content and style.

My thanks are also extended to Kim Duey, Scott Estep, Steve Estep, Dean Flemming, Geoff Kunselman, Greg Mason, and Joe McLamb, who read the initial manuscript and offered helpful suggestions, to my great benefit.

Mark Brown, Bonnie Perry, and Rene McFarland at The Foundry Publishing are a team that blesses the church and those who resource the church. Audra Spiven provided careful attention in the editing of the book.

I have had the blessing of writing while engaged in a living laboratory of leadership, serving the Church of the Nazarene as an overseer for the Kansas City district. More than 100 congregations and 550 credentialed clergy allow me opportunities to put into practice what I am learning from the apostle Paul. Many of the individuals I serve are accomplished leaders, and I learn more from them than they learn from me. To all of them I offer my profound gratitude for the privilege of serving with them.

INTRODUCTION
THE C'S OF LEADERSHIP

Here is a trustworthy saying: Whoever aspires
to be an overseer desires a noble task.
—1 Timothy 3:1

Aside from Jesus Christ, it is hard to imagine that anyone else has had more impact on Christianity than the apostle Paul. Of course, the key to the effectiveness of the church—then and now—is not a remarkably gifted individual. The key to the effectiveness of any church is almighty God. But movements begin with individuals, and God uses Paul to initiate the spread of Christianity.

Paul provides so much for so many: for the theologian, a doctrinal construct; for the preacher, a message; for the missionary, a strategy; for the entrepreneur, a model; and, for the student of leadership, a wealth of leadership lessons and examples for consideration. Excellent leadership qualities are woven through Paul's life and ministry. Richard Ascough and Charles Cotton claim that Paul essentially "wrote the book" on transformational leadership.[1]

Unfortunately, Paul gets a bad rap these days from some who view him as intimidating, abusive, discriminatory, and offensive. He was viewed the same way by some in his own day. There is certainly enough material in the New Testament to allow the serious reader to make up her or his own mind on the matter. I'll be drawing from both firsthand accounts (the thirteen New Testament letters that claim Paul as the author) and secondhand accounts (Luke's perspective in Acts) in this treatment.

Ever adapting to new circumstances and generating new ideas, Paul's leadership style is incarnational—he lives among the people to whom he ministers and writes. In Paul, one finds leadership genius—passion, strategy, relational capital, vision. Some leaders pray daily for wisdom, grace, and stamina. Paul has all three in abundance.

The C's

Many years ago, I became aware of the C's of ministry—a list of qualities that could be used to evaluate ministers being considered for pastoral staff positions in the church I was serving. They included:

- **Call**: Does this person have a keen sense that they have been invited to vocationally participate in God's redemptive work in the world?
- **Character**: Is this a person of integrity?
- **Competence**: Does this person have the skill set to do what we are asking and expecting?
- **Consistency**: What is this person's prior record of faithfulness and fruitfulness?
- **Chemistry**: How will this person mesh with the existing team?[2]

Upon becoming an overseer in the denomination I serve, I discovered the C's also provide a helpful framework for evaluating women and men seeking ordination and preparing to give themselves to a lifetime of service to the Lord and his church, as well as for assessing ministers being considered as pastoral candidates in local churches.

As I began to research Paul's leadership style, it occurred to me that these C's of leadership—with some adaptations—provide a fitting structure from which to construct a study of Paul's leadership. Paul's **call, connections, character, competencies,** and **challenges** supply an appropriate framework for consideration.

There are a couple of things to note before we begin. First, for the sake of convenience and consistency, I will use "Paul" throughout the book, rather than switching back and forth between his early name, Saul, and his later name, Paul.

Second, this is not intended to be a theological book, although that is difficult to avoid when considering Paul's writings. Nor is it intended to be a biblical survey, though Paul's and Luke's New Testament writings are the documents of the research. It is intended to be a book on leadership—Paul's leadership. There is much to learn about leadership from Paul. Let's dive in.

PART 1

THE LEADER'S CALL
How a Leader Is Prepared
and Summoned

*I thank Christ Jesus our Lord, who has given me strength, that he
considered me trustworthy, appointing me to his service.*
—1 *Timothy 1:12*

*More and more it seems to me that about the best thing in life is
to have a piece of work worth doing and then to do it well.*
—*Theodore Roosevelt*[1]

A leader's development is often marked by discernible progression.
Metaphors can be helpful in describing this progression, including
a seasonal description of a leader's development in terms of spring,
summer, autumn, and winter. Another helpful metaphor comes
from sports: preseason, season opener, mid-season, late season, post-
season (retirement). The terms *learning, leading,* and *leaving a legacy*
also provide a description of healthy leadership development.

In my own leadership, I can look back at how a progression of
assignments led to specific parts of my development. In the first assignment I learned to lead; in the second assignment I actually led;
in the third assignment I learned to lead *with* others; in the fourth
assignment I learned to lead *through* others.

Paul's development as a leader also follows a discernible arc, marked by both places and opportunities. We turn now to that marked progression.

— ONE —

CHILD OF TARSUS: PRELUDE TO LEADERSHIP

Paul answered, "I am a Jew, from Tarsus in Cilicia,
a citizen of no ordinary city.
Please let me speak to the people."
—Acts 21:39

Paul's hometown is no backwoods burg. Tarsus has considerable importance economically and militarily and has become a blend of various civilizations kept at peace under the rule of Rome. Strategically located near a seaport and on a major east-west trade route, the city attracts a diverse mix of international culture and commerce from caravans carrying goods from the Far East to Rome. "Paul was reared amid the busy streets and crowded bazaars of Tarsus," suggests F. B. Meyer, "thronged with the merchants, students, and sailors from all parts of the world."[1] Tarsus is the principal city of the Cilician province. Situated between the mountains and the sea, it lies ten miles inland on the river Cydnus in the southeast corner of modern Turkey. The city stands in a rich and luxuriant plain. To the north rise the snow-capped Taurus mountains. The Mediterranean lies out-of-sight, a half-day's walk to the south.

Leaders are influenced by heritage, early environment, and upbringing, and Paul is no different. Although he is Jewish, Paul's upbringing in Tarsus enables him to understand and connect with gentiles. While living in a strict and ordered home environment, Paul grows up aware of how the rest of the world works, speaks, behaves, and reasons. He is accustomed to interactions with both Greeks and Romans. Likely Paul speaks Greek—the common language of trade—from his earliest years, has a working knowledge of Latin, learns Hebrew in the synagogue, and speaks Aramaic—the language of Judea (and Jesus)—at home. N. T. Wright observes, "We can safely assume, then, that Saul grew up in a cheerfully strict observant Jewish home, on the one hand, and in a polyglot, multicultural, multiethnic working environment on the other."[2]

Since Tarsus is not a Jewish city but a Roman one, the Jewish inhabitants most likely all live in the same neighborhood, which for them provides an island of purity in a sea of the profane. Living close to one another offers safety and makes it convenient to observe the same religious celebrations and obtain kosher food. Such proximity also helps keep the Jews religiously "in line" because life is lived in full view of their neighbors.

Leadership Lesson: **A leader's worldview and cultural awareness will naturally be shaped by where that leader is born and raised.**

Paul's initial perspective will be significantly shaped by his childhood context. In addition to being immersed in Jewish culture, Tarsus provides Saul with opportunities to observe multiple other cultures too. Hometown values influence all of us to one degree or another—sometimes positively, sometimes negatively. For some, those values provide a foundation of appreciation for healthy cross-cultural relationships. For others, those values produce at best a narrow understanding of multicultural richness or, at worst, outright prejudice.

. . . circumcised on the eighth day, of the people of Israel . . .
—*Philippians 3:5a*

Paul is probably a little younger than Jesus of Nazareth, likely born in the first decade of what we now call the first century.[3] He is born to strictly observant Jewish parents who ensure their son is circumcised on the eighth day, as required by the Jewish law.

The Torah commands ritual circumcision of all male Jews, a necessity for admittance to the temple and to synagogues. The commitment to circumcision dates back to God's covenant with Abraham in Genesis 17:10–14. While there are health benefits associated with circumcision, the practice is primarily a visible sign of the covenant and a continual reminder of their heritage. God's chosen people are to be marked, and it is the duty of a Jewish father to have his son circumcised.

This religious rite becomes a point of contention in the early church, and Paul will extensively address the challenging issue in his writings.

. . . of the tribe of Benjamin . . .
—*Philippians 3:5b*

Paul is named eight days after his birth, when he is circumcised. His parents' choice to name him Saul can be traced to his tribal connection. The name is given in honor of the most famous of the Benjamites, King Saul, the first king of Israel. Paul is named as a reminder of his heritage as a member of the tribe of Benjamin—a heritage that Paul never forgets. Years later, he will write to the church in Rome, "I am an Israelite myself, a descendant of Abraham, from the tribe of Benjamin" (Romans 11:1).

His parents apparently also give their son the Roman name "Paul." He is called Paul for the first time in the Bible in Acts 13, when he is on the island of Cyprus. Luke, the writer of Acts, indicates that the names are interchangeable—"Saul, who was also called Paul" (v. 9)—and refers to him as Paul through the remainder of Acts. And, of course, Paul identifies *himself* as Paul in the many New Testament letters he writes to the various churches he pastors. It is fitting that the one who will become the apostle to the gentiles uses his gentile name.

> *. . . a Hebrew of Hebrews; in regard to the law, a Pharisee.*
> —Philippians 3:5c

Paul comes from pure Hebrew stock. His parents are Pharisees, the Jewish party that is most fervent in Jewish nationalism and adherence to the law of Moses. "They lived with a fierce, joyful strictness in obedience to the ancestral traditions. They did their best to urge other Jews to do the same."[4] Purity is a priority for the Pharisees, who seek to guard their offspring against contamination from anything or anyone non-kosher. The family likely retains the Hebrew language in a gentile environment.[5]

The Pharisees exercise great care in observing the Sabbath law and food restrictions. They scrupulously tithe the produce of the soil and refuse to eat food that is subject to tithe unless the tithe has actually been paid. They hold to a bodily resurrection. Because of their meticulous adherence to the laws of purity and to tithing, they do not associate easily with those who do not adhere. Later in life, Paul tells King Agrippa that he has lived as a Pharisee, the strictest party of the Jewish religion (Acts 26:5).

In our day, "Pharisee" has become a synonym for religious pride and even hypocrisy, but in Paul's day, the Pharisees represent some of the noblest traditions of the Hebrew people, and being one is a badge of honor. There are always cultural pressures that will tempt devout Jews to compromise, but Paul's people are marked by zeal for Israel's God, zeal for Israel's Torah, and zeal for Israel's purity. Paul himself can claim to be "faultless" with regard to "righteousness based on the law" (Philippians 3:6).

Leadership Lesson: The identity and traditions a leader learns in childhood create a foundational awareness that becomes strongly ingrained.

As children, the stories we hear, the sights we see, the songs we sing, and the habits we learn become shaping influences in our lives. Attitudes develop as knowledge and experience are gained. This will be especially true of Paul, who grows up in a home that is intentionally structured and strongly opinionated about faith and life.

Nothing is known of Paul's mother. He never mentions her. Perhaps she dies early in Paul's life, and that is why he views Rufus's mother as his own (Romans 16:13). Nor does Paul ever mention a wife. Some speculate that he *was* married but that his wife left him after his conversion to Christianity. He has at least one sister because he has a nephew who will play a prominent role in Paul's deliverance from an assassination plot (Acts 23:12–22).

> *And because he was a tentmaker as they were,*
> *he stayed and worked with them.*
> *—Acts 18:3*

Every Jewish boy is taught a trade, usually that of his father. Paul's father is most likely a master tentmaker. Among the industries in Tarsus is a thriving textile business, producing material made from goats' hair. This becomes the basis of the family business, in which Paul is apprenticed and will practice even after leaving Tarsus. The tents made in Tarsus are used by caravans, nomads, and armies. The family business makes interaction with other cultures necessary, also contributing to Paul's awareness of language and culture.

Throughout his ministry, Paul will earn his own living in the family business. Tentmaking is a portable trade, suitable for an itinerant life. Weaving a dark, coarse cloth from goats' hair will require a loom but not an established workshop. As long as he has his working tools, Paul can set up shop in any town.

Leadership Lesson: Co-vocational (or bivocational) ministry—when the minister gains additional income from another job—continues to be an option and sometimes a necessity for many ministers today.

In my own leadership context, the number of co-vocational ministers is on the rise as pastors seek additional employment for financial or missional reasons. Such ministers are following in Paul's footsteps. Although it may ease financial burdens for both the minister and the church, co-vocational ministry can also increase time-management burdens for the minister and the minister's family. However, many ministers report increased fulfillment from the opportunity to engage the mission field through additional employment. They cite increased ministry effectiveness as a byproduct of their co-vocational status. Churches are blessed by these faithful and hard-working pastors.

This man is a Roman citizen.
—Acts 22:26b

Paul's childhood provides him the best of two cultures. Not only is he raised with the heritage and traditions of a Jewish family, but he also has Roman citizenship, something he will occasionally use to his advantage. Paul's father is apparently a Roman citizen. As Roman citizens, the family's status will be coveted.

Although it is unknown exactly how Paul's family became citizens of Rome, F. F. Bruce suggests that perhaps Paul's father, grandfather, or great-grandfather performed some outstanding service to the Roman cause.[6] Paul's status as a Roman citizen by birth will benefit him greatly as he travels on his missionary journeys. He will use his citizenship to escape flogging in Acts 22 and appeal to Caesar in Acts 25.

F. B. Meyer observes that in Tarsus, "Paul became equipped with the prerequisites of a great traveler."[7] For this there are three necessary conditions: speech, safety, and sustenance. Greek is the common language of the world, and Paul will become as familiar with Greek as he is with Hebrew. All the world is Roman. To be a Roman citizen gives Paul a measure of safety in his travels. It is like having a global passport with significant rights attached. As for sustenance, as long as there are goats nearby, Paul can provide for himself. There will always be demand for the coarse cloth he can produce.

Leadership Lesson: **God is at work from the beginning in the lives of those whom he calls, preparing them to serve him well.**

God uses it all. Our background and early experiences are made useful for his work. Ascough and Cotton write, "Paul believed that his genetic code, his upbringing, and his training in religion were all part of God's plan and were intended to lead up to the moment when God would call him to a specific task."[8] J. Oswald Sanders calls Paul "a world-citizen—a Jew living in a Greek city, and with Roman citizenship. Both by birth and by training Paul possessed the tenacity of the Jew, the culture of the Greek, and the practicality of the Roman, and these qualities allowed him to adapt to the polyglot peoples among whom he was to move."[9] Growing up in Tarsus gives Paul a multicultural understanding that enables him to contextualize the gospel effectively in his later ministry.[10] May we all recognize that God can use our genetics, upbringing, and training for his glory. God can use any beginning to bring about his perfect end.[11]

Questions for Leadership Development

1. In what ways has your upbringing—your heritage, traditions, and early environment—prepared you for leadership?

2. How has your worldview been shaped by your hometown?

3. If you don't have one already, what would be your tentmaking trade—your non-ministry co-vocation?

4. How has your life begun to counter your cultural conditioning?

TWO

CHILD OF JERUSALEM: EDUCATION

I am a Jew, born in Tarsus of Cilicia, but brought up in this city [Jerusalem]. I studied under Gamaliel and was thoroughly trained in the law of our ancestors. I was just as zealous for God as any of you are today.
—Acts 22:3

Paul's promise as a student of Jewish law becomes evident at an early age as he applies himself to learning the Torah in the synagogue at Tarsus. As is the case in many cities today, students from Tarsus often leave the city to continue their studies in other places. This is exactly what Paul does. By the age of thirteen, Paul's knowledge of Jewish history and Scripture is sufficient to allow him to continue the next phase of his education.

Paul's parents make certain he has an orthodox upbringing by arranging for him to spend his formative years in Jerusalem. They likely see Jerusalem as being not only the place to shape Paul's intellectual stature but also the place for Paul "to be immunized against the infection of the Hellenistic world."[1] So, as a young teen, Paul is sent to Jerusalem to continue his formal education and begin his study for the office of rabbi. He has already shown the aptitude and propensity for it, so off to Jerusalem he goes, "his head full of Torah and his heart full of zeal."[2] Perhaps it is reasonable to speculate that Paul's sister is already married, living in Jerusalem, and can provide the lodging he will need.

Leadership Lesson: **Where we are educated, and who educates us, are important factors in a leader's development.**

Educational institutions serve a noble and valuable purpose and can contribute significantly to the development of a leader. Such institutions have values, perspectives, and agendas that influence what is taught and how. It befits students to be aware of these dynamics and to make educational choices accordingly. Where we are educated, who educates us, and whom we are educated with all matter a great deal.

The Teaching of Gamaliel

Paul is not just a child of Tarsus; he is also a child of Jerusalem—literally and figuratively. In later years, he refers to Jerusalem as the place he was reared. In Jerusalem, Paul sits at the feet of Gamaliel for his formal training in Jewish law. To study the Torah in the shadow of the temple is quite a heady experience for a Jewish boy. For five or six years, Paul is schooled in the Hebrew Scriptures and the disciplines of logic by the most respected rabbi of that era. Rabbis are part teacher and part lawyer, and they serve as the spiritual and religious teachers of Jewish communities. Once rabbis complete their own academic preparation, they are usually ordained by the rabbi under whom they studied.

Gamaliel is a noted authority on religious law—perhaps *the* authority in Paul's day. He probably leads the School of Hillel, since he is the grandson of the great Rabbi Hillel. According to tradition, Gamaliel's interpretation of Scripture—which he holds to be wholly inspired by God—reflects an attitude of compassion toward people.

Despite his renown, relatively few of his teachings are preserved, in part because his opponents in the House of Shammai seem to have gained control of the Sanhedrin (the highest Jewish council) after his death.

Luke introduces Gamaliel as an influential Pharisee and celebrated teacher of Mosaic Law—a man held in great esteem by all the people (Acts 5:34). He is also a key member of the Sanhedrin. The council is composed of seventy-one members—a mixture of Sadducees and Pharisees—and has religious and judicial authority.

The Sanhedrin has commanded the apostles not to preach in the name of Jesus (Acts 4:18). But the apostles continue to preach, teach, and even perform miracles in Jesus's name. In fact, we read in Acts 5 that the early Christian church experiences significant growth in numbers and great effectiveness in ministry during this time—which does not sit well with the high priest and the Sadducees. Driven by jealousy, they throw the apostles into prison. But that very night, God's angel goes to the prison and frees them and then commands the apostles to go and preach in the temple (Acts 5:19–20). The apostles promptly obey.

Leadership Lesson: **Jealousy will seriously undermine leadership.**

The actions of the Sadducees are motivated primarily by their envy. Jealousy—either *from* a leader or *about* a leader—will negatively impact the culture of any organization. When jealousy is present, agendas are corrupted, and decisions are made emotionally, rather than sensibly. The end result is that self-interest is protected and promoted, rather than the good of the whole.

The next morning, the high priest calls the Sanhedrin together to deal with the issue but discovers that the apostles are not in prison and are again preaching in Jesus's name—and, what's worse, *in* the temple! Peter and the other apostles are brought before the Sanhedrin for the crime of continuing to preach the gospel despite being expressly prohibited. The Sanhedrin, infuriated by the apostles' obstinacy, proposes to kill them. That's when Gamaliel steps up.

Gamaliel provides a voice of reason, encouraging the Sanhedrin not to rush into judgment or act rashly. He offers calm reasoning and wise intervention, encouraging his fellow Pharisees to reconsider their intended action. Gamaliel uses his influence and presents an argument against killing the apostles, reminding them of the previous revolts of Theudas and Judas of Galilee, which collapsed quickly after the deaths of those individuals. Gamaliel concludes with this advice: "Therefore, in the present case I advise you: Leave these men alone! Let them go! For if their purpose or activity is of human origin, it will fail. But if it is from God, you will not be able to stop these men; you will only find yourselves fighting against God" (Acts 5:38–39).

Leadership Lesson: **Taking an opposing stand in a highly charged, emotional situation requires tact, reason, knowledge, and wisdom.**

Gamaliel's stand against the murderous Sanhedrin is effective. He is already respected, and he expresses himself with conviction. One of the things Gamaliel does is move to have the apostles put outside. He does not want to expose the discussions of the council to non-members, an act that shows his respect for the council, increasing his credibility. This decision also eliminates any posturing that would likely take place by members of the Sanhedrin, were the apostles present. He gives good advice, asking the Sanhedrin to take heed but not forcing his views on them. It is a sincere request that invites the council to reevaluate their decision and draws their attention to the rest of his argument. It requires courage to speak against the Sanhedrin. They could easily turn on him. But Gamaliel is fearless, and he provides an example of how to persuade a difficult crowd. Often young leaders, or leaders early in their tenure, do not yet have the credibility of a longstanding, proven leader like Gamaliel. In these cases, respect, tact, reason, knowledge, and wisdom like those shown by Gamaliel become even more important, along with courage.

Eventually, the Jewish leaders give in to Gamaliel's advice and agree to follow his wise counsel. Though they beat the apostles, they do not kill them. The council then releases the apostles after again giving them strict orders not to speak in the name of Jesus.

Leadership Lesson: **Sometimes deliverance comes from unexpected places.**

When situations become dire, even hopeless, God is still sovereign, working all circumstances out for his ultimate glory. God often chooses unlikely persons to accomplish his will. He uses Gamaliel, a member of the Sanhedrin, to deliver Peter and the apostles. This providence would not be lost on Paul.

The Example of Stephen

Learning takes place both inside and outside the classroom, and Paul's outside-the-classroom encounter with Stephen—who was likely about the same age as Paul—will contribute greatly to his education in Jerusalem.

Stephen is first mentioned in Acts 6 as one of the Greek-speaking, Hellenistic Jews selected to participate in a fairer distribution of food and aid to the Greek-speaking widows. He is described as being "full of the Spirit and wisdom," "full of faith and of the Holy Spirit," and "full of God's grace and power," a man who "performed great wonders and signs among the people" (Acts 6:3, 5, 8).

Stephen's teaching angers some members of one of the Jerusalem synagogues. When they challenge him, they become incensed when Stephen bests them in debate. Furious at this humiliation, they bribe witnesses to provide false testimony that Stephen has blasphemed, and he is then dragged before the Sanhedrin. It is not known whether Paul is at this time a member of the Sanhedrin, but he is most surely present for the trial. As the proceedings begin, the false witnesses spin their lies and stoke the fiery anger of the Sanhedrin. In contrast, Stephen, unruffled, appears to have "the face of an angel" (v. 15), and as a result the eyes of the members of the Sanhedrin are laser-focused on him.

When he is given the opportunity to respond, Stephen answers with a long speech that comprises most of Acts 7. F. B. Meyer observes that Stephen provides "the first attempt to read the story of God's dealings with Israel in the light of Christ" and "the earliest commentary on the Old Testament by the New."[3] Stephen presents his view of the history of Israel, beginning with Abraham then focusing primarily on Moses. He then moves to address Israel's disobedience of God, which culminated in the crucifixion of Jesus, and is now seen in the actions of the Sanhedrin. At this bold accusation the council becomes incensed and rushes Stephen out of the city to be stoned.

Leadership Lesson: Leaders are called to "speak prophetic truth with tender grace."[4]

Stephen models this in an exceptional way as he speaks to the Sanhedrin. J. D. Greear observes, "One minute he is pointing his finger at the religious leaders and calling them heartless murderers (truth) and the next—as they are stoning him—he prays for their forgiveness (grace)."[5] As in Stephen's day, our society today finds such leaders to be—in the words of Greear—a "befuddling contradiction." Sadly, speaking the truth with grace will not keep some from scratching their heads and others from hating you. A gentle answer doesn't always turn away wrath, and when it doesn't, Stephen shows us how to respond in a way that has a profound impact on Paul.

In a judicial stoning, the first stones must be thrown by those who bring the charges. Needing freedom of movement in order to throw the stones, the witnesses strip off their outer coats and toss them to Paul, who holds the garments during the execution. In the face of their rage, Stephen's reaction is bewildering. He lifts his shining face toward heaven and prays, "Lord Jesus, receive my spirit" (7:59) as the mob completes what the witnesses began.

And Paul watches in approval.

Leadership Lesson: Faithfulness sometimes results in martyrdom.

Stephen does everything right, yet he ends up being the first martyr of Christianity. His most effective contribution to the kingdom of God isn't his sterling service to the church or his passionate speech. His most effective contribution is his martyrdom—the sacrifice of his life for his Lord. Since the persecution and martyrdom of Christians continues today in some parts of the world, we pray for those who face such challenges.

Stephen's death—especially the way he dies—powerfully affects Paul. It is not the fact of the death that troubles him; it is the light on the martyr's face—the words, the patience, the forgiveness—that Paul will never forget. He has "the face of an angel." And Stephen prays in the same way Jesus prayed from the cross, asking for mercy for his executioners.

But Stephen's witness does not soften Paul's heart—it hardens it. The persecution of the followers of Jesus begins in earnest on the day of Stephen's death. Though Paul is young, his leadership potential is recognized. He must be one of Gamaliel's most promising students—strong, passionate, clear in thought, deliberate in speech, decisive in action. Paul is given a leadership role in the Sanhedrin's campaign against the Christians. He will give himself entirely to the stamping out of this treason, going from house to house arresting Christians in Jerusalem.

Though blood is literally in Stephen's mouth, Paul has figuratively tasted it himself. And the taste of that blood will propel him to Damascus.

Questions for Leadership Development

1. How did you choose where you would be educated?

2. Who have been your most influential teachers? What made them influential?

3. How have your fellow learners influenced your education?

4. Have there been times when you have been sincere—but wrong? How can you be certain your sincere action is right?

5. Why are the decisions of some leaders motivated by jealousy? Has that ever happened to you?

6. What can we learn about the art of persuasion from Gamaliel's speech to the Sanhedrin?

7. What enables Stephen to show such courage in his defense before the Sanhedrin?

THREE

CHILD OF DAMASCUS: TRANSFORMATION

Meanwhile, Saul was still breathing out murderous threats against the Lord's disciples. He went to the high priest and asked him for letters to the synagogues in Damascus, so that if he found any there who belonged to the Way, whether men or women, he might take them as prisoners to Jerusalem. As he neared Damascus on his journey, suddenly a light from heaven flashed around him.
—Acts 9:1–3

In Jerusalem, the followers of Jesus are giving the religious establishment fits. The Jesus movement is gaining significant momentum, and many feel that if drastic measures are not taken to suppress it, things will get hopelessly out of hand. Paul, by now a well-trained student of Jewish law, believes that throwing the apostles in prison is the best strategy to prevent the further spread of the gospel. The harassment of Christians becomes intense.

Acts 9 opens with Paul persecuting the followers of "the Way." The violence of the persecution drives many of the disciples out of Jerusalem. As the Christians begin to scatter, Paul goes to the high priest with a request. Not content to persecute Christians in Jerusalem only, Paul asks for legal papers to pursue the Jews who have fled to Damascus, more than two hundred miles north of Jerusalem. He asks for official letters to the synagogues, authorizing him to arrest men or women who follow the Way, and to bring them to Jerusalem for punishment. Paul has essentially become a terrorist in the name of God.

A Transforming Journey

Early one morning Paul sets off for Damascus, his head full of Scripture and his heart full of hate. Warrants in hand, his mission is to arrest religious refugees. "No doubt hoping," writes F. F. Bruce, "that if he could accomplish this purpose satisfactorily in Damascus, he could repeat the procedure in other foreign cities."[1] Paul will have plenty of time to plan his strategy and sharpen his resolve. He is likely riding a donkey, on what is probably a five- or six-day journey. Unlike Balaam's beast (see Numbers 22), Paul's donkey will not stop him but will bear him to a divine appointment.

Leadership Lesson: Transforming journeys are seldom understood to be that at the beginning.

Sometimes, when you look a little closer at things, you discover that what is actually going on isn't exactly what you thought was going on. Paul thinks he is going to Damascus to persecute Christians. He is mistaken. Unbeknownst to Paul, this trip to Damascus is going to change his life forever. Perhaps the journey you are presently on will also be a transforming journey.

A Transforming Moment

As Paul is headed to Damascus to arrest the followers of Jesus, he himself is arrested *by* Jesus. With astonishing suddenness, the persecutor of the followers of the Way becomes a follower of the Way himself. This sudden transformation occurs when he encounters the crucified Jesus, now exalted as risen Lord. At about noon, as Paul is nearing Damascus, a great light suddenly flashes from the sky, "brighter than the sun, blazing around me and my companions" (Acts 26:13). Paul and his fellow travelers fall to the ground.

A voice is heard in Aramaic, "Saul, Saul, why do you persecute me?" (9:4; 26:14). Even as Paul asks, "Who are you, Lord?" (9:5; 26:15), he knows the answer. The discovery is both terrifying and tremendous. The followers of Christ have been right all along, and Paul has been terribly wrong. He is instantly aware of two things: First, Jesus is alive. Second, Jesus is the Way. The voice continues, "I am Jesus, whom you are persecuting" (9:5; 26:15).

In Paul's trial before King Agrippa, he tells Agrippa that Jesus also said, "It is hard for you to kick against the goads." A goad is what a farmer uses to prod cattle or oxen. It is a long, slender stick, blunt on one end and pointed on the other. The farmer holds the blunt end and uses the pointed end to urge oxen to action. Sometimes the oxen kick at the goad, which only increases their pain and discomfort.

Jesus instructs Paul to get up and go into Damascus to await further instructions, and his surrender to the Lordship of Jesus Christ is immediate and absolute.

Leadership Lesson: A transforming moment can forever change a leader's life.

That day on the road to Damascus, Paul encounters the divine in a way that changes everything—his perspective, his heart, his direction, his mind, his purpose for living. He experiences a thorough transformation. Paul is completely converted by Jesus Christ. It is the decisive moment of his life. His zeal is not changed, just redirected. Augustine calls Paul's conversion "the violent capture of a rebel's will."[2] Paul's thinking does a U-turn. He changes his mind about Jesus, about the resurrection, and about the followers of the Way. Many people in this sort of situation resort to clinging desperately to their old views, no matter how overwhelming the evidence that those views are not correct. This mistake causes leaders to compound the error rather than acknowledge the need for a course correction and be open to the transformation that results. Paul's willingness to make this intellectual, emotional, and spiritual shift is remarkable.[3]

The testimony of others is not what wins Paul's heart. It is the one thing that could convince Paul that Jesus is indeed the risen Lord—Jesus reveals himself to Paul. "We are only Christians," writes Benedict XVI, "if we encounter Christ."[4] The risen Lord confronts Paul and overwhelms him with love, forgiveness, and grace.

If the importance of an event can be determined by the amount of space given to it in Scripture, then the conversion of Paul is second in the New Testament only to the resurrection of Jesus. It is described three times in Acts (see chapters 9; 22; 26). Addressing the significance of Paul's conversion, Bruce writes, "No single event, apart from the Christ event itself, has proven so determinant for the course of Christian history as the conversion and commissioning of Paul."[5] That he has seen Jesus will become one of Paul's deepest convictions.

A Transforming Mission

Paul is blinded by the transforming moment on the outskirts of Damascus. In the city, he spends the next three days praying and fasting. One can only imagine what those three days in darkness are like for Paul—the opportunity for reflection, the sense of transformation, the awareness of the cruelty and inhumanity of the persecution he has propagated.

It is unknown whether any of Paul's traveling companions—no doubt also committed to the task of persecuting Christians—also experience transformation on the Damascus road. If not, they are likely eager to get Paul off their hands. Now blind and difficult to travel with, and having done what must appear to them to be a confused about-face in his thinking, Paul becomes a liability. Needing to find a place to ditch him in Damascus before they head back to Jerusalem with their bewildering report, they make their way to Straight Street, to the house of a man named Judas. Perhaps Judas is a Jewish merchant of means, already identified as a suitable host for a representative of the Sanhedrin. At this home, Paul finds himself in the unfamiliar position of dependence. The proud, self-sufficient Pharisee is now a humbled and disabled believer in Jesus.

Paul's last sight before he went blind was of Jesus. Captured Hebrew kings were often made blind by their enemies, who ensured the last sight they saw was of a loved one being put to death. The last sight Paul saw before becoming blind was of the one he will *begin* to love: Jesus. Rather than seeing someone alive put to death, Paul saw the one who was put to death, now alive.

Meanwhile, in Damascus, there is a disciple named Ananias. Just when Paul most needs a friend, Ananias enters the picture. God gives Ananias a vision and a mission. In his vision, Ananias is directed by the Lord to go to a house he has never visited, owned by a man he has likely never met, to meet another man he likely hoped never to encounter. Very little is known of Ananias. As far as we know, he is not a preacher, teacher, evangelist, or missionary. The Bible simply identifies him as a disciple living in Damascus who has a vision.

First, God calls Ananias by name. Then God gives him specific directions—"Go to the house of Judas on Straight Street"—followed by specific instructions to "ask for a man from Tarsus named Saul" (Acts 9:11). God has a mission for Ananias.

Leadership Lesson: **There are times when God gives leaders specific directions and specific instructions.**

One of the many ways God reveals himself in the Old and New Testaments is through visions. Today, God most often speaks to us through his Word and his Spirit. The gift of discernment enables leaders to determine whether God is giving specific directions and instructions.

Ananias is reluctant and begins to question God. He's not rebellious; he's cautious. He wants to verify that he has heard correctly. Ananias has questions about this man Paul, and he wants to be certain God knows everything *he* knows about Paul—the history, reputation, and risks linked with Paul. Questioning is not always rebelling. Ananias is saying, "Lord, did I hear you right? Last I heard, Paul was hunting down Christians and throwing us in prison. It's hard to believe Paul is now a follower of the Way!" Ananias does not only have questions about the man, but he also has questions about the mission. "Lord, you want me to go lay hands on Paul? He came to town to lay hands on people like me!"

Leadership Lesson: **God loves hard cases!**

And God loves people and churches who are willing to be a grace-place for hard cases. Is there anyone you think God can't transform? Perhaps you've thought, *He's too far gone,* or, *Her heart is too hard.* No matter how misguided one has become, or how intentional the harm brought to others, no one is beyond hope. Regardless of what a person may have done, no one is out of reach of the grace of God. Ananias doesn't realize God is already working on the other side of the equation. Scales will fall from two people's eyes that day in Damascus—Paul's and Ananias's. This mission is going to move Ananias out of his comfort zone.

Ananias is told three things about Paul: first, that Paul is praying; second, that Paul is a "chosen instrument" (9:15) to take the gospel message to the world; third, that Paul will suffer for Jesus's sake. And Ananias is told, "Go!" (v. 15). In spite of his earlier reservations, he does what God asks him to do. Ananias knows all about Paul, but God has a mission, so he goes without delay, without fear, walking right into the house of Judas. Ananias also goes without a grudge, greeting Paul as a brother.

Leadership Lesson: Leaders are often given a specific mission, the accomplishment of which is completely dependent on their willingness to engage.

What if Ananias had refused? Did God have someone else prepared? We don't know. We don't know if Ananias was God's first or fifth choice. Perhaps there is not always someone else standing in the wings who can accomplish the mission God has prepared and equipped us to do. Perhaps some things go undone. Or maybe the wrong people do them. What a tragic loss it would have been if Ananias had not been willing to do what God was calling him to do. The Ananiases of this world serve in relative obscurity, doing precisely what God asks them to do and going to the places God asks them to go.

Ananias lays his hands on Paul to bless him and to pray for him. Paul recovers his sight, instantly and completely, as what appear to be scales fall from his eyes. Note what happens next. Paul is baptized, and he is filled with the Holy Spirit. He joins the fellowship and is invited to the potluck that follows the service.

Leadership Lesson: **Nothing makes more of a difference in a leader's life than being filled with the Holy Spirit.**

It certainly makes a difference in Paul, who is now inwardly equipped to be a fully devoted follower of Jesus Christ. What flows out of Paul's life—his sermons, his travels, his writings—is evidence of the remarkable change that occurs when he is filled with the Holy Spirit. Education is no substitute for being filled with the Spirit. Nor are experience, gifting, or abilities a substitute for being filled with the Spirit. Being filled with the Spirit enables leaders to serve with the power of God at work in their lives.

Paul, newly and deeply transformed, experiences a new power and a new direction. Immediately, he begins preaching about Christ. The newly baptized Paul goes at once to the synagogue in Damascus and begins to proclaim that Jesus is the Son of God. The Jewish community is shocked and offended; as a result, Paul will soon be on the road again.

Leadership Lesson: **People like Paul need people like Ananias.**[6]

Ananias provides Paul with just what he needs at that moment—a prayer for his physical healing, an opportunity to be baptized, and an invitation to join the fellowship of believers. Emerging leaders often need someone to extend the blessing of fellowship and acceptance.

Questions for Leadership Development

1. Which resonates more with you—the concept of a transforming *journey* or a transforming *moment*? Why?

2. Have you had a "Damascus road" experience? If so, describe it, and how it transformed your approach to leadership.

3. Can you identify goads that God has used, or is using, in your life?

4. Like Ananias, has the Lord ever given you specific instructions or directions that produced unexpected results? Explain.

5. Has God ever asked you to do something that moved you out of your comfort zone? What was your response?

6. What difference does being filled with the Spirit make in a leader's life?

— FOUR —

CHILD OF ARABIA: PREPARATION

But when God, who set me apart from my mother's womb and called me by his grace, was pleased to reveal his Son in me so that I might preach him among the Gentiles, my immediate response was not to consult any human being. I did not go up to Jerusalem to see those who were apostles before I was, but I went into Arabia. Later I returned to Damascus.
—Galatians 1:15–17

Soon after his conversion, Paul makes his way to Arabia to reflect on his new situation and perhaps commune with God in the same way and place other biblical leaders connected with God in days gone by. N. T. Wright suggests that Paul goes to Arabia because that's where Mount Sinai is located. Mount Sinai is where God came down in fire and gave Moses the Torah. "Sinai was also where Elijah had gone when it all went horribly wrong. Sinai was where Paul went for the same reason."[1] Paul's Arabian sojourn lasts three years (Galatians 1:18) and takes place in the desert of the Sinai Peninsula, a barren wilderness. Due south of Damascus, the area is sparsely populated with stark physical features. Paul is likely alone most of this time.

Leadership Lesson: Solitude can be of great benefit to leaders.

Almost every significant leader in the Bible spends time in solitude and obscurity, including Joseph, Moses, David, and Elijah. Solitude provides fertile soil for reflection—an important component in the formation of a leader. Reflection results in formation when lessons are thoughtfully applied to the current realities of life and leadership. Reflection is a powerful yet often underutilized tool in a leader's toolbelt. Investing time in reflection serves leaders well, allowing the development of patterns of thoughtful response rather than careless reaction.

Perhaps Paul believes he needs to spend as much time with Jesus as the disciples did. So he stays in Arabia for three years. Scripture is silent about what Paul does in Arabia. No doubt, during these years, Paul studies the Hebrew Scriptures in light of Jesus and develops a robust theology, allowing the Spirit to recalibrate his thinking. Like putting on corrective lenses for the first time, Paul now sees everything differently, and he is eager to explore Scripture with new eyes.

Paul likely prays, studies, ponders. He soaks in reflection on Scripture in light of his newfound faith in Christ. N. T. Wright suggests,

> If you had asked Saul of Tarsus, before the meeting on the road to Damascus, where Israel's story and God's story came together, the two natural answers would have been the temple and the Torah. The temple indicated that Israel's God desired to live in the midst of his people; the Torah, that he would address his people with his life-transforming word. Paul now came to see that both these answers pointed beyond themselves to Jesus and of course to the Spirit.[2]

The centrality of Christ replaces the centrality of the Torah in Paul's thought as he studies intently.

Paul's formation differs widely from that of his fellow apostles. They traveled the dusty roads of Judea and Galilee with Jesus and were educated at his feet. They came to know Jesus intimately *before* the resurrection. Conversely, Paul knows *of* Jesus, of his ministry, of his death. But he comes to *know* Jesus only *after* the resurrection. Paul goes to Arabia to learn *from* the risen Jesus, not just *about* him. He claims to have learned directly from Jesus by revelation (Galatians 1:11–12). That learning happens in Arabia.

Paul's education and conversion have prepared him for this season of formation. In Arabia, his soul and character are formed for a lifetime of leadership and service.

Leadership Lesson: Every leader needs a season (or seasons) of formation.

Paul has significant education and has experienced conversion, but now formation is needed. Education can provide a solid foundation, but leaders usually need something more than education to be adequately prepared to serve well. Sometimes it is an internship or a position where one can learn from a wise, experienced, seasoned leader. Always, it is an opportunity to reflect, learn, and grow deep roots. Formation is accomplished in seasons of reflection, when the lessons of education are internalized, personalized, and owned in light of the realities of the vocation to which the leader is called. For Paul, this means reflecting on and recalibrating his understanding of Torah in light of Jesus the Messiah.

Paul grows deep roots in the desert of Arabia. His days are filled with discovery as his significant understanding of the law gains new perspective in light of grace. He begins to see Jesus throughout the Old Testament and is able to connect Jesus with many Old Testament prophecies. Scripture takes on fresh vibrancy and greater depth in light of Jesus. Many Pauline scholars think this was also a time of missionary activity.[3] Paul has already received his commission to preach among the gentiles, and he started proclaiming the gospel in the synagogue in Damascus days, if not hours, after receiving that commission.

Leadership Lesson: **Seasons of formation build deep leaders.**

The deep roots Paul is able to grow in Arabia will sustain him in difficult times. Growing deep roots allow leaders to develop a strength of character that holds them steady when the storms of life threaten to topple them, and enables them to tap into deep reservoirs of sustaining grace.

Back to Damascus

Although the Bible is not explicitly clear on the exact timeline, it appears that after Arabia, Paul revisits Damascus and Jerusalem before returning to Tarsus (see Galatians 1:17–21). In this retracing of his steps, we see the beginning of another pattern in Paul's ministry. Paul will often retrace his steps on his missionary journeys.

In Damascus, Paul immediately begins preaching in the synagogues. He experiences early success, but then the backlash is violent and hateful. The Jewish leaders want to do away with him, and he finds himself in imminent danger. The disciples come to his rescue when the Jewish leaders determine to murder him. Leaving the city through the city gates will mean certain death, since the gates are watched with plans to kill Paul when he tries to escape. So the disciples sneak him out of town by lowering him over a wall at night, using a rope and a basket (Acts 9:20–25). The irony will not be lost on him—Paul, who originally set out for Damascus boldly, with Jewish power and authority, will leave Damascus cautiously, wholly dependent on the help of the very ones he originally planned to harm.

Back to Jerusalem

Fleeing Damascus, Paul returns to Jerusalem, where the disciples are troubled by his appearance and provide a less-than-warm welcome. "They were all afraid of him," writes Luke, "not believing that he really was a disciple" (Acts 9:26). Rejected by the Jewish leaders in Damascus, Paul is now rejected by the Christ-following disciples in Jerusalem. A pattern of rejection is developing that will be repeated often in the course of Paul's ministry.

But in Jerusalem, one person steps up to help him. Barnabas comes to his rescue and becomes his advocate. This timely new friend intercedes for Paul and makes the introductions needed for Paul to be accepted. According to Luke, Barnabas brings Paul and the leaders of the Jerusalem church together (v. 27).

Leadership Lesson: Every Paul needs a Barnabas.

You either need someone to be Barnabas in your life, or someone needs you to be Barnabas in their life. If you aren't the one benefiting from the gracious introduction, perhaps you need to be the one making the gracious introduction, paving the way for someone who has been rejected or ostracized. Perhaps someone who has changed for the better needs an advocate who encourages others to believe the transformation is genuine. Maybe you know someone who needs a second chance, and you can be the one to provide it.

In Jerusalem Paul wants to meet Peter, the leading apostle. Paul desires not just to make Peter's acquaintance but also to learn from him the details of Jesus's ministry and the tradition of the teaching that originates with him. Paul dug deep into Scripture in Arabia, but since he was not acquainted with Jesus before the resurrection, he longs to hear firsthand accounts. He spends fifteen days with Peter in Jerusalem, taking a crash course in the life of Jesus, listening and learning as much from Peter as he can of Jesus's ministry while he walked the earth.

Paul does not meet any of the other apostles during this visit except "James, the Lord's brother" (Galatians 1:19). What he is not able to learn from Peter, he learns from James.

As short as Paul's visit is, it is long enough for his life to be threatened. This time, the murder plot is hatched by the Hellenistic Jewish leaders (Acts 9:29).[4] These may be some of Paul's old associates who mounted the attack on Stephen. Undoubtedly, they now regard their lost leader as a traitor to the cause. Once again, people are angry enough at Paul to want to kill him, so the disciples hustle him out of Jerusalem and escort him down to the sea at Caesarea. From there they will put Paul on a boat back to Tarsus.

While it is beginning to look like Paul is going to be a hard man to keep alive, in time it will become apparent that Paul is instead going to be a hard man to kill.

Back to Tarsus

Once Paul is hustled out of Jerusalem and off to Tarsus to escape the assassination plot, we do not hear of him for the next several years. He is likely plying his tentmaking trade in Tarsus. These are silent years for Paul. He is waiting, continuing to reflect, and possibly beginning to dream. His heart, soul, and mind are being tempered for the adventure that awaits.

Leadership Lesson: "Exceptional work is often preceded by extended waiting."[5]

Leaders sometimes find themselves in a waiting mode. You are educated, prepared, and willing, yet you find yourself on the shelf for a season. You are not assigned, not being used, not contributing like you long to be. British author James Stalker observes, "Waiting is a common instrument of providential discipline to those to whom exceptional work has been appointed."[6] Jesus waited thirty years before his ministry begins. God often prepares us with seasons of waiting. These times allow for our wills to be broken, our skills to be honed, and our character to be shaped. When you are on the Potter's wheel, the Potter is seldom in a hurry. You may be weary of waiting. Hang in there. Wait on the Lord. If you are called and gifted, you will be discovered. God will make sure that happens. At just the right time—in the fullness of time—your time will come. When God does finally open the door, and the call comes, it is often unexpected. But that invitation to serve always comes in God's timely providence. God is not only preparing you for the opportunity, but he is also preparing the opportunity for you. And when both ends of the equation are ready, the call will come.

Leadership Lesson: **True development is both more painful and far slower than most people want to admit.**[7]

We do not know Paul's age when he encounters Christ for the first time, when he returns to Tarsus after his conversion, or when he sets out on his missionary journeys. It appears he converts as an emerging leader in Judaism, so he is probably in his early thirties. He then spends what most people would call his "best years" toiling in Arabia and then Tarsus in almost complete isolation from the church. By the time he starts his missionary work, he is well past his prime by contemporary standards. This is an important but often overlooked aspect of his leadership. Paul has a brief experience of glory as a rising Pharisee, then fades into obscurity, and finally gets called off the bench at a point in his life when many leaders begin thinking about their own mortality. Contrast that approach to leadership development (the Crockpot method—requiring years, if not decades, of slow heating) to the modern versions of leadership development offered on bookshelves today (the microwave method).

Back in Tarsus, Paul will toil in his tentmaking trade in an environment that deflates any delusions of grandeur, likely facing rejection from family and former friends. God is shaping him for a season of significant ministry, though it is likely difficult for him to realize at the time. God is preparing him for the next step. At just the right time, Paul will be summoned to Antioch. And that time is coming.

Questions for Leadership Development

1. What are the benefits of solitude?

2. Can you identify a season of formation in your life?

3. Why are deep roots important for leaders?

4. Who have been the Barnabases in your life?

5. When have you been a Barnabas for someone else? Or for whom *could* you be a Barnabas?

6. Why do leaders sometimes find it difficult to wait on the Lord?

FIVE

CHILD OF ANTIOCH: ORDINATION

Now in the church at Antioch there were prophets and
teachers: Barnabas, Simeon called Niger, Lucius of Cyrene,
Manaen (who had been brought up with Herod the tetrarch)
and Saul. While they were worshiping the Lord and fasting,
the Holy Spirit said, "Set apart for me Barnabas and
Saul for the work to which I have called them."
So after they had fasted and prayed, they placed
their hands on them and sent them off.
—Acts 13:1–3

Antioch of Syria is the third-largest city in the Roman Empire. Only Rome in Italy and Alexandria in Egypt are larger. Antioch (current-day Antakya, Turkey) is situated on the Orontes River approximately twenty miles inland from the Mediterranean Sea and about three hundred miles north of Jerusalem. On the trade route between China in the east and Rome in the west, it is a busy seaport trade hub, possessing a lively mix of people from different cultures and religions with high intellectual and political status.

According to Acts 11, the Christian community at Antioch begins when the intense persecution that breaks out in Jerusalem after the death of Stephen prompts a number of Jewish disciples to flee to Antioch. These Jewish believers preach exclusively to fellow Jews in the city. They are joined by Christians from Cyprus and Cyrene who migrate to Antioch and preach primarily to the Greeks. Both these groups believe in Jesus and are gathered into the first multicultural congregation in the history of the Christian church.

The leaders of the Jerusalem church seem to exercise control, or at least provide direction, over the spread of the gospel. When they hear of the considerable number of gentile conversions taking place in Antioch, they send a delegate to see what is going on and to minister to the growing congregation (see Acts 11:19–26). The man sent is Barnabas—"the encourager."

Barnabas arrives in Antioch, quickly sizes up the situation, and realizes he needs help. He discovers a large and growing church in Antioch that has as many gentiles by birth as Jews. The group needs to become firmly established in Scripture and understand that Jesus the Messiah is the fulfillment of those scriptures. Given this situation, Barnabas begins to see the need for a colleague to share in the responsibility of supervising the life and ministry of the new church. There are skills and gifts that Barnabas lacks to resource the growth of the church. But Barnabas knows someone with those skills—Paul—and he travels 150 miles around the northeast tip of the Mediterranean to Tarsus to persuade Paul to return to Antioch with him (Acts 11:25).

Paul, who was under the tutelage of the Spirit in Arabia, now finds himself under the tutelage of Barnabas in Antioch. Together, they will teach the mixed assembly of Jewish and gentile believers for a whole year (v. 26).

Leadership Lesson: **An emerging leader's opportunity to have an experienced leader mentor or coach them is a tremendous gift.**

One of the strongest factors of success and fulfillment in leadership is the opportunity to learn from an experienced and effective leader. Paul's opportunity to serve with Barnabas will allow him to observe not only what Barnabas does but also how he does it. Barnabas becomes a sounding board for Paul's questions, providing an objective and experienced perspective. Internships, shadowing, and being coached or mentored by effective leaders provide valuable leadership development opportunities for leaders today. Barnabas serves as Paul's strategic sponsor, which is more than a mentor. A strategic sponsor can not only provide a great example and sound advice, but the sponsor also has the power to influence a young leader's assignments, making sure they get the correct blend of experiences to round out character and competence. Most great leaders have had a strategic sponsor, and in most cases, they found this person by working for or with them. Like a true strategic sponsor, Barnabas opens key doors in Paul's developmental journey and coaches Paul through them. Being a strategic sponsor is tough business because it is similar to being a parent in that one must endure the young leader's growing pains.[1]

During the ministry of Paul and Barnabas, the Spirit breaks out in Antioch, and God's work flourishes. At Antioch the believers are called Christians for the first time (Acts 11:26). Both Jewish and gentile believers are enjoying the fellowship of the church. F. B. Meyer notes the wonder of the phenomenon: "They ate together without question; and even Peter, when on a visit to Antioch, was so charmed with the godly simplicity and beauty of their communion, that he joined freely with them, and partook of their love feasts and common meals."[2] Antioch is the one place in the world where Christian gentiles are living in harmony and unity with Christian Jews.

About this time, a Christian prophet from Jerusalem comes to Antioch and foretells of a great famine that will strike the Roman world. The compassionate Christians in Antioch respond to the prophecy with generous offerings to help the Jerusalem church survive the scarcity. Barnabas and Paul are tasked with the mission of carrying these gifts to the elders in Jerusalem (Acts 11:27–30).

Leadership Lesson: **Generosity blesses not only those who receive but also those who give.**

There is likely a strong connection between the Antioch church and the Jerusalem church, from which many of the Antioch believers have come. Despite the likelihood of Antioch also being affected by the famine, they freely share from their abundance. Not only is it an act of generosity, but it is also a symbol of the unity and interdependence of Jews and gentiles in the church. Their generosity and the strengthening of the connection may be a factor when the Council of Jerusalem meets a few years later to consider the matter of circumcision for gentile believers. The decision will prove to benefit the church at Antioch. Perhaps in the providence of God, the generosity of the church in Antioch will not only be a present blessing to the Jerusalem church but also, in some unexpected way, provide a future blessing to the Antioch church.

When Barnabas and Paul return from Jerusalem, they bring Barnabas's cousin with them. John Mark is a young man who is eager to join them in the work. Other young believers are also being developed as God continues to bless the church in Antioch. The church is rich in leadership. In addition to Barnabas and Paul, there is Lucius of Cyrene, Manaen, and Simeon, who also goes by Niger (Acts 13:1). The church is a center of evangelism, discipleship, and leadership development, and it will soon become a center of mission.

Sensitive to the leading of Holy Spirit, the church at Antioch becomes aware that God may have other plans for Paul and Barnabas. The growing church wants to see other cities experience what they are experiencing. They desire to see people in other places believe in Christ and grow in their faith, and they determine that the best way to accomplish this mission is to send missionaries to evangelize other cities. It is obvious to all that Barnabas and Paul have the gifts, graces, and passion to accomplish this task as missionaries to the gentiles. In Acts 13, Paul and Barnabas are "set apart" for the first missionary journey (vv. 2–3).

Leadership Lesson: **Leaders would do well to have a loose grip on gifted and graced leaders under their care.**

God may have plans for these leaders that take them to other places. Some leaders become angry and sullen when they learn that someone they are overseeing has an opportunity to serve elsewhere. Rather than resenting the circumstance, the leaders in Antioch bless Paul and Barnabas. As soon as they realize God is calling Paul and Barnabas, they release them with a blessing. We should be willing to do the same for those God is calling. The modern mission movement has its origin in Antioch because the church is willing to send its best and brightest. There will be others engaged in gentile evangelism but none with Paul's strategic planning and dynamic energy.[3] There is no selfish clinging by the church, no spirit of suspicion, no whining about their loss. Paul and Barnabas are blessed, affirmed, supported, and encouraged. Too many churches, and too many church leaders, cling too tightly, lacking the grace to release. A loose grip is an affirmation of trust in God's providence and God's will. Some leaders have a hard time letting go and sending high-capacity leaders to serve where they are most needed. Selfish leaders grip in order to control and possess; generous leaders release to freely serve. Leaders with a loose grip can train and equip young leaders with the intention of sending them. A mature leader can find a sense of healthy pride in seeing the development in a young leader released to expand the kingdom of God.[4]

Christianity's first missionary expedition is launched from Antioch. Organized Christian global mission work has its beginning when Barnabas and Paul are set aside by the leading of the Holy Spirit and then sent out from the church in Antioch. The Antioch church becomes the first sending church when the believers lay their hands on Paul and Barnabas, bless them for the work ahead, and send them off to accomplish the mission, accompanied by John Mark (Acts 12:25–13:3).

Leadership Lesson: **For Christian ministers, being commissioned to achieve the mission is a significant and meaningful act.**

God has already called and commissioned Paul on the Damascus road, but now the church confirms and affirms that call and commission. The church in Antioch has confidence to send Paul, and he begins his missionary journeys with the assurance that both God and the church have commissioned him. God calls; the church confirms that call. In the church today, ordination is a powerful aspect of the commissioning of women and men for ministerial leadership. The denomination I serve strongly links ordination and leadership: "God calls and gifts certain men and women for ministerial leadership in the church. . . . Ordination is the authenticating, authorizing act of the church, which recognizes and confirms God's call to ministerial leadership as stewards and proclaimers of the gospel and the church of Jesus Christ."[5] Ordinands complete requirements of education, experience, and character. In the same way, Paul has completed significant education, displayed gifts and graces for ministry during his time in Antioch, and his character is found to be above reproach.

Antioch will be both the starting and ending point for Paul's first missionary journey. Paul and Barnabas will return to report on the fruit of their journey, sharing everything God has done in their travels (Acts 14:26–27). They tell the story, beginning with their arrival in Cyprus to their last stop in Pisidian Antioch. During the trip, Paul emerges not only as the primary spokesman (replacing Barnabas) but also with a new name (Acts 13:9). They will have covered more than a thousand miles on foot, and Paul will have significantly more scars when he returns than when he left.

Leadership Lesson: The importance of a leader's report cannot be overstated.

It is essential for leaders to communicate the results of their work—the fruit of the commissioning. The report of a leader is important not only because of the information shared but also because of the accountability modeled. Even today, missionaries continue the practice Paul began of returning home on deputation, or home assignment, to report back to the churches who sent them.

Paul's development as a leader is clearly seen in Antioch. The progress in his development takes place in stages. Stage 1 is Paul being identified as an emerging leader by Barnabas, who recruits him to serve in Antioch. Stage 2 is Paul's internship as he serves with Barnabas. Stage 3 is Paul and Barnabas being sent together to Jerusalem, representing the church at Antioch. Stage 4 is team-building with the addition of John Mark. Stage 5 is deployment, with Barnabas and Paul being sent to evangelize gentiles. Stage 6 is reporting and accountability. Stage 7 is follow-up (Paul's letters to the churches he plants), which is perhaps the stage where leaders most often fail.[6]

Paul will end his second missionary journey in Antioch and begin his third from there. Halfway through Luke's narrative in Acts, the center of interest shifts from the mother church in Jerusalem to the sending church in Antioch. F. F. Bruce writes of Antioch, "If the church of Jerusalem was the mother church of Christians in general, the church in Antioch was the mother church of gentile Christians in particular."[7]

As Paul begins his missionary journeys, and then writes letters to the churches he has started, to the churches he intends to visit, and to the young ministers he mentors, we begin to clearly see in his words and actions the character of a leader.

Questions for Leadership Development

1. What blessings have you received from generosity—both your own and others'?

2. Do you tend to have a loose grip or tight grip on the leaders under your care?

3. Have you ever been commissioned for a significant mission?

4. What are the benefits of leaders reporting to their constituencies?

5. To what degree do you recognize God's role in your leadership opportunity?

PART 2

THE LEADER'S CONNECTIONS

The Relationships That Enrich and Expand a Leader's Effectiveness

I thank my God every time I remember you. In all my prayers for all of you, I always pray with joy because of your partnership in the gospel from the first day until now.

—Philippians 1:3–5

I think if I've learned anything about friendship, it's to hang in, stay connected, fight for them, and let them fight for you. Don't walk away, don't be distracted, don't be too busy or tired, don't take them for granted. Friends are part of the glue that holds life and faith together. Powerful stuff.

—Jon Katz[1]

Journeys change us. Those changes are often brought about more by the companions who accompany us and the connections we make along the way than by the journey itself. In Part 2 we will consider the scope and impact of Paul's network of traveling companions, ministry colleagues, and providential contacts.

Effective leaders are typically highly relational individuals who develop significant connections both inside and outside the organizations in which they serve. Because it is difficult for a person to be connected except through personal relationship, connections to a business, organization, or ministry are always relational. The strength of the relationship determines the strength of the connection.

Paul is continually making connections on his missionary journeys, carefully developing a network of significant relationships. These relationships are critical to the establishment of churches across Asia Minor and to Paul's leadership. There are significant challenges in building these communities of faith, which is why establishing relationships will be an enduring priority.

Paul succeeds in his missionary endeavors due in large part to the network of Christian brothers and sisters he establishes. As a connected leader, he tenaciously stays in touch with fragile groups in hostile contexts. He is relationally wealthy. In Romans 16 alone, he sends greetings to more than thirty individuals—members of a church he has not yet visited! Between eighty and ninety people are described as Paul's coworkers in Acts and the New Testament letters attributed to him. Some appear to relate to Paul as peers, others as subordinates. Some work closely with Paul, others independently. Some carry out their work primarily in a local setting, and others travel with Paul or serve as his delegates when he cannot travel. All of his coworkers act cooperatively with him in a wide variety of mission activities.

— SIX —

FIRST-CIRCLE CONNECTIONS: TRAVELING COMPANIONS

*The two of them [Barnabas and Paul],
sent on their way by the Holy Spirit, went down
to Seleucia and sailed from there to Cyprus.*
—Acts 13:4

Barnabas
The Gift of Encouragement and the
Disappointment of Separation

Tod Bolsinger suggests that there are three kinds of people who contribute significantly to the well-being of leaders. The people who
care more about the mission than they care about the leader are
partners. The people who care more about the leader than they do
about the mission are friends. The people who care about the leader
for the sake of the mission are mentors.[1] Paul's mentor is Barnabas.

Barnabas is a Cypriot, a native of Cyprus. Barnabas isn't his original name. His actual name is Joseph, but he is such an inspirer that
the disciples in Jerusalem find it natural to call him Barnabas, which
means "son of encouragement." Barnabas has the gift of enabling
others to flourish, which will greatly benefit Paul in his development
as a leader.

Leadership Lesson: **Individuals and organizations need all the encouragement they can get.**

People who provide encouragement greatly benefit individuals *and* groups. In the world of professional sports, teammates who are encouragers are called clubhouse leaders. They have the ability to change the atmosphere for the better. Their presence typically increases morale because they help people feel better about themselves and others. Leaders like this are equally valuable in business and ministry contexts. Such encouragers have a gracious presence that produces a climate of inspiration and mutual support that enable both individuals and organizations to realize greater potential.

Barnabas first appears in Luke's narrative as a generous contributor to the general fund set up in the early Jerusalem church (Acts 4:36–37). Graciously reaching out to the downtrodden and needy, Barnabas supplies all the encouragement he can whenever he finds a person or cause needing a boost. Even after his conversion, Paul is still feared by the disciples in Jerusalem. When Paul sorely needs a friend in Jerusalem, Barnabas fills the role—much like Ananias did in Damascus.

Leadership Lesson: **Emerging leaders often need an advocate to vouch for them.**

When a respected leader gives you credibility by standing with you, doors may begin to open that were previously shut. This is what happens to Paul when Barnabas befriends him. Leaders benefit when there is a Barnabas in their life.

In Acts 11, news reaches the disciples in Jerusalem that Greeks in Antioch are being saved through the ministry of evangelists from

Cyprus and Cyrene. Since Barnabas is from Cyprus, the apostles send him to Antioch, realizing that his awareness of the culture and language will enable him to minister effectively and encourage them.

As the church continues to grow in Antioch, Barnabas travels to Tarsus to recruit Paul to help him with the developing ministry. For a year, Barnabas mentors Paul in leadership and ministry. When Paul and Barnabas are sent to Jerusalem to deliver an offering given by the church in Antioch for the needy saints in Jerusalem, they return with John Mark, a young leader who joins the ministry team in Antioch. And when Paul and Barnabas are commissioned by the church at Antioch to evangelize the gentiles, they take John Mark with them on the first missionary journey.

Early in the journey, John Mark abruptly abandons the mission and returns to Jerusalem. We don't know if he is homesick, or if he is intimidated by the journey ahead, or if he deserts them for some other reason. Perhaps he is comfortable with Barnabas being the leader of the group but uncomfortable when Paul assumes that position. We do know that his departure leaves Paul with a lingering sense of betrayal and suspicion. Later, when Paul suggests launching another missionary trip, Barnabas—the encourager and includer—wants to give John Mark a second chance. Paul adamantly refuses. He believes John Mark has proven his unreliability by abandoning them on the first journey.

This point of contention will result in a rift and Paul ultimately falling out with Barnabas.[2] N. T. Wright suggests that, as a traveling companion, Paul "must have been exhilarating when things were going well, and exasperating when they weren't."[3] Barnabas may find it intolerable that Paul would question his judgement, especially since Barnabas has encouraged others to give Paul a second chance.

At the end of Acts 15, there arises "such a sharp disagreement that they parted company" (v. 39), and not amicably. It is hard to imagine two spiritual giants—gifted, mature, theologically astute, proven partners—having an argument that leads to separation. But that is what happens. They permanently separate due to irreconcilable differences, and as far as we know, their paths never cross again. Barnabas and John Mark sail away to Cyprus. Paul chooses a different companion for himself for his second missionary journey. Silas, a Roman citizen, will accompany him "through Syria and Cilicia, strengthening the churches" (v. 41).

Silas
The Other Voice in Prison Duets

When Paul sets out from Antioch on his second missionary journey, his fellow traveler is Silas (or Silvanus), a member of the Jerusalem church. Silas is a seasoned disciple and a Roman citizen. Prior to joining Paul, Silas is sent as an emissary to Antioch, along with Judas, to present the report from the Jerusalem Council concerning the matter of circumcision (v. 32). Silas obviously has credibility with the Jerusalem church, and the diplomatic advantage of having a Jerusalem Christian as his traveling companion is likely not lost on Paul.

Well into their journey, Paul and Silas are thrown into prison at Philippi, a Roman colony in Macedonia, after being stripped and beaten with rods. Their crime is delivering an evil spirit out of a fortune-telling slave—a miracle that has financial implications for her owners. At midnight in the prison, their feet in stocks, Paul and Silas are praying and singing hymns when an earthquake sends the doors of the prison flying open. When he realizes the prisoners under his charge have had the ability to escape, the jailer is about to kill himself when Paul assures him all the prisoners are still there in the jail. The relieved jailer cares for their wounds and then is baptized, along with his household.

At daybreak, Paul and Silas are released by the magistrates, who do not realize Paul's status; they are filled with dread and angst when they learn of his Roman citizenship. Public beating and imprisonment may be common punishment for noncitizens, but it certainly is not for Roman citizens. The whole incident ends with a public apology and a request that Paul and Silas leave town.

Leadership Lesson: Some of the greatest joys in leadership come from the relationships with those who accompany leaders on the journey.

Traveling companions are those who generally know you best, see you in a variety of circumstances (good and bad), and with whom you share significant experiences. Paul and Silas likely never forgot their shared experience in the Philippian jail. When situations become challenging, a companion on the journey can be a ready source of encouragement, counsel, and fellowship. Shared experiences contribute to the strengthening of relationships.

According to Acts 17–19, Silas and Timothy travel with Paul from Philippi to Thessalonica, where they are treated with hostility by some jealous Jews. The harassers follow the trio to Berea, threatening Paul's safety, and causing Paul to separate from Silas and Timothy. Paul travels to Athens, and Silas and Timothy later join him in Corinth. After Corinth, Silas does not again appear as Paul's traveling companion. He does appear in the salutation of 1 and 2 Thessalonians, where he is listed along with Paul and Timothy as a coauthor of both letters. He is also mentioned in 1 Peter 5:12 and may have served as Peter's scribe.

Timothy
The Protégé

Timothy appears to have been one of the converts during Paul and Barnabas's visit to Lystra on the first missionary journey. When Paul returns a few years later with Silas, Timothy is already a respected member of the Christian congregation, as are his grandmother Lois and his mother, Eunice, both noted for their piety and faith (see 2 Timothy 1:5).

Paul is impressed with Timothy's teachable spirit, his love for God's truth, and his faith-filled heritage. His qualities and gifts are admirable, and Paul recognizes in young Timothy the makings of a great leader for the church. Paul invites him to join the missionary team, and when Timothy accepts, he is apprenticed to Paul in his apostolic ministry.

Timothy's mother is Jewish, but his father is Greek, so Timothy is not circumcised. In order that he might serve most effectively, Paul proposes that Timothy undergo the rite to ensure his acceptability to the Jews they will be evangelizing (Acts 16:3). Timothy is circumcised not because it is mandatory but so there might not be an obstacle to admission to the Jewish synagogues.

Because of Timothy's close relationship with Paul, we learn more about him than we do of Paul's other traveling companions. Timothy is said to have been acquainted with the Hebrew Scriptures since childhood. It could be inferred from 1 Corinthians 16:10 that he is by nature reserved and timid. He has a weak stomach, and may be subject to ill health or frequent ailments. He is prone to nervousness yet endures hardship without flinching. Paul warns him to flee youthful lusts, and will testify that Timothy is without self-interest.

Paul will trust Timothy with important assignments and delicate missions. He sends Timothy to Macedonia with Erastus, perhaps to prepare Paul's intended journey to Jerusalem (Acts 19:21–22), with the aim that he will eventually arrive at Corinth. Timothy arrives at Corinth about the same time that Paul's first letter reaches the city. The letter is not well received, and Timothy quickly returns to Ephesus to report this to Paul.

Timothy is with Paul when Paul sends his letter to the Romans (Romans 16:21). Paul then proposes sending Timothy to the church in Philippi (Philippians 2:19–23), and Timothy delivers a monetary gift from the Philippians when Paul is at Corinth. Paul will leave Timothy at Ephesus to govern that church and will write letters to Timothy to provide encouragement and pastoral counsel.

Timothy's name appears as the coauthor of 2 Corinthians, Philippians, Colossians, 1 Thessalonians, 2 Thessalonians, and Philemon. Paul has significant confidence in Timothy and writes to the Philippians, "I have no one else like him" (2:20). When Paul is in prison and awaiting martyrdom, he summons his faithful friend Timothy for a last farewell.

Leadership Lesson: Emerging leaders need experienced leaders to mentor them.

Emerging leaders best learn from someone worthy of emulation. Most great leaders owe the honing of their leadership skills to the influence of a mentor. For an emerging leader like Timothy, receiving the investment of an experienced leader like Paul is a priceless gift. Timothy is Paul's son-in-the-faith, the heir of Paul's mantle of leadership. As they journey together, Timothy will learn Paul's heart, theology, habits, strategy, and leadership, which will significantly influence Timothy's development as a leader.

Luke
When Your Physician Is Your Friend

Luke becomes Paul's traveling companion in Troas, during the second missionary journey. The addition of a medical doctor to the traveling missionary team will be a tremendous blessing. Paul already has scars from Philippi, bruises from Lystra, and wounds from Berea. Like tattoos marking significant experiences, Paul's wounds are visible reminders of the cities he has visited.

Luke becomes Paul's constant companion, his personal physician, and one of the closest and dearly loved of Paul's fellow workers (see Colossians 4:14). His name is included in the greetings in three of Paul's letters—Colossians, Philemon, and 2 Timothy. Luke is a trusted and faithful friend who acts as a physician, personal aide, and secretary to Paul, and—under the inspiration of the Holy Spirit—as a historian for the church.

Leadership Lesson: **Leaders are often gifted in multiple areas.**

Luke is a physician, a historian, and an author. I remember suddenly becoming aware as a teenager that our pastor wasn't just a good preacher but was also significantly gifted in other areas, notably construction. Ministry leaders today are often multi-gifted in a multiplicity of fields and skillsets.

Luke is a historian and careful scholar, keeping a log of the events of the journey with a physician's strict regard for accuracy. He tells the story of Paul's first journey in Acts 13–14. During Paul's second missionary journey, Luke's writing switches from "they" to "we," apparently signaling that he joins Paul, Silas, and Timothy at Troas. Luke also joins Paul at the end of his third missionary journey and accompanies him to Jerusalem. In Acts 27, the narrative shifts, and Luke begins writing in the first person again, suggesting that he experiences the shipwreck, accompanies Paul on the journey to Rome, and is with him to the last. Luke's presence in Rome with the apostle near the end of Paul's life is confirmed by 2 Timothy 4:11: "Only Luke is with me."

Leadership Lesson: Even if your vocation calls for you to stay in one place, growing and developing as a leader is always a journey on which we need trusted companions.

Not everyone will have an itinerant vocation like Paul's. Nevertheless, leadership is still a journey, and our need of traveling companions is just as significant and important. Companions help share the load, lift spirits, and give counsel and advice based on their perspective and wisdom. Choose wisely whom your traveling companions will be. Do not attempt to go the journey alone.

Questions for Leadership Development

1. Why are traveling companions important?

2. Who have been your closest companions on your leadership journey?

3. Who has been a son or daughter of encouragement in your life?

4. To whom have you been a son or daughter of encouragement?

5. Have you ever experienced a conflict that led to separation? How might you have handled it in a way that could have led to healthy resolution?

6. If you were to choose a traveling companion on the basis of one gift or ability, what would that one gift or ability be?

SEVEN

SECOND-CIRCLE CONNECTIONS: MINISTRY COLLEAGUES

I thank my God every time I remember you. In all my prayers for all of you, I always pray with joy because of your partnership in the gospel from the first day until now.
—Philippians 1:3–5

Paul is committed to teamwork and the development of ministry colleagues. When he establishes a church, he identifies and trains local leaders to work in cooperation with him. Paul's ministry colleagues assist him in his preaching and teaching ministry, in addressing problems in the churches, in his travels, in writing letters, and in meeting his needs in prison. He instructs these leaders in person when present and by letter when absent. A pattern of sending is established early in the churches Paul establishes, and some of Paul's ministry colleagues are sent to serve in strategic places to keep the work strong.

Paul's relational strength is especially seen in Romans 15:23–24: "But now that there is no more place for me to work in these regions, and since I have been longing for many years to visit you, I plan to do so when I go to Spain. I hope to see you while passing through and to have you assist me on my journey there, after I have enjoyed your company for a while." Note the importance of the word "after." First comes the relationship, then the partnership in ministry.

Priscilla and Aquila

Paul has no two finer friends and ministry colleagues than Aquila and Priscilla, a Jewish couple who come from Pontus, on the shore of the Black Sea in ancient Turkey. They live in Rome until Claudius expels the Jews from that city, then immigrate to Corinth (Acts 18:1–2), where they meet Paul during his second missionary journey.

Leadership Lesson: Immigration—the movement of people brought about by persecution, war, weather disaster, or economic reasons—provides opportunities for both the well-being of the immigrant and for the spread of the gospel in the host country.

This lesson is as evident in Paul's day as it is in ours. In Paul's day the movement of Christians is brought about primarily by persecution. In the modern era, significant movement takes place around the world. Many immigrants have been instrumental in the spread of the gospel, despite the huge challenges and insecurities they may face in their new situations.

Like Paul, Priscilla and Aquila are tentmakers, and they apparently strike up an instant friendship, becoming fellow workers in both tentmaking and disciple-making. Paul stays in Corinth for some time, and when he is ready to leave, Aquila and Priscilla accompany him to Ephesus to set up their tentmaking business and prepare to evangelize the city (Acts 18:18–19). Paul continues on to Jerusalem and then to Antioch.

Leadership Lesson: Married couples can have highly effective leadership partnerships.

The combined abilities of spouses often provide a comprehensive balance, making for a significantly gifted team. In my work, there is an observable increase in spouses serving as co-pastors as churches realize the significant gift of such leadership teams. This is a fairly recent development, almost unheard of a generation ago. The primary leadership role should not be determined by gender but by ability. Of the six times Aquila and Priscilla are mentioned in the New Testament, four times Priscilla's name is mentioned first, which is significant for its countercultural aspect. Such primacy indicates her important ministry role. F. F. Bruce observes, "More often than not Priscilla is named before her husband; this may suggest that she was the more impressive personality of the two."[1]

While ministering in Ephesus, Priscilla and Aquila hear Apollos speak in the synagogue. Apollos is a brilliant Jew from Alexandria and an impressive speaker. However, he has only a rudimentary knowledge of Jesus. Priscilla and Aquila invite him into their home and teach and mentor Apollos toward maturity, filling in the missing gaps of his understanding of the gospel (Acts 18:26).

Leadership Lesson: Investing in emerging leaders may be the most significant and lasting contribution made by experienced leaders.

Apollos is able to become an important leader in Corinth because Priscilla and Aquila take the time to invest in him and prepare him for a significant leadership opportunity.

Paul encourages Apollos to go to Corinth before Apollos is willing (1 Corinthians 16:12). When Apollos does leave Ephesus for Corinth, he goes with a letter of introduction from the Ephesian believers, who also recognize how valuable such a minister will be in Corinth. His eloquence impresses the believers in Corinth, and his ministry becomes more appealing for many than Paul's ministry. Some members even believe that Apollos, not Paul, is the leader they need.

Priscilla and Aquila are living in Rome when Paul writes the letter to the Romans and sends them greetings as his "co-workers in Christ Jesus" (16:3). When Paul writes 1 Corinthians, he sends greetings on behalf of Priscilla and Aquila and "the church that meets at their house" (1 Corinthians 16:19), indicating Priscilla and Aquila are in Ephesus, from where Paul is writing.

Titus

Titus travels with Barnabas and Paul to Jerusalem and becomes the test case for circumcision when the Jerusalem Council meets (Galatians 2:1–5). He is Greek, not Jewish, and some say Titus needs to be circumcised—in other words, become fully Jewish—before he can become a Christian. (One wonders whom the church may be trying to metaphorically circumcise these days.) Barnabas and Paul stand firm against this, and Titus is spared.

Paul sends Titus to Corinth to remedy the fallout caused by Paul's first letter to the Corinthians and the disastrous follow-up visit during which Paul's leadership and authority are challenged. Titus is to return not to Ephesus, from where he was sent, but to Troas, where Paul anticipates meeting him. Paul is alarmed when Titus does not show up in Troas and relieved when they finally link up in Macedonia (2 Corinthians 2:13; 7:6). Titus brings good news. The church in Corinth has taken Paul in the right spirit, has treated Titus well, and longs to see Paul again. The apostle is overjoyed with the news of Titus's success. He writes 2 Corinthians in response, and Titus is dispatched back to Corinth with the letter. Paul will eventually join Titus in Corinth.

Leadership Lesson: Troubleshooters and peacemakers are gifts to leaders.

Some leaders have a propensity to rub people the wrong way. When Paul does this with the Corinthians, he dispatches Titus to smooth things over. Titus has the grace, wisdom, and diplomacy to repair the fractured relationship and bring peace and understanding to the situation. Sometimes a leader's emissary can accomplish what needs to be done better than the leader can.

When Paul plants a church and leaves to go on to the next region, he appoints someone he trusts to equip the church, train other leaders, and provide leadership. After Paul preaches in Crete, he ordains Titus as bishop of the island, an indication of the esteem he has for Titus. Titus seems to flourish in new and challenging circumstances. Paul's letter to Titus is one of the three pastoral epistles (along with 1 and 2 Timothy) that Paul writes to describe the requirements and duties of overseers and to encourage this leader Paul has appointed.

Titus will later be spotted in Dalmatia (2 Timothy 4:10), a Roman province situated northwest of Macedonia and due north of the bootheel of Italy, on the Adriatic Sea, where Paul sends Titus to preach the gospel, likely after meeting him in Nicopolis (Titus 3:12).

Tychicus

Tychicus, who is mentioned five times in Scripture, could be called Paul's personal courier. He is often dispatched by the apostle to carry his letters to the churches. He is sent to carry Paul's letter to the Ephesian church (Ephesians 6:21–22). He is sent, along with Onesimus, to deliver Paul's letter to the Colossian church (Colossians 4:7–9). He is probably the one tasked with delivering Paul's letter to Titus in Crete (Titus 3:12). Since Paul is in prison when he writes these letters, Tychicus delivers vital personal messages to churches and individuals whom Paul cannot visit himself.

Leadership Lesson: **The people who ensure that good communication takes place are incredibly important to leaders.**

In Paul's day, Tychicus is the person who literally delivers the written communication to the intended recipients. In our day, similar roles are played by persons responsible for information technology, organizational communication, and even by the person who proofreads a leader's correspondence. In both Ephesians and Colossians, Paul explains that Tychicus is also being sent to encourage the church and answer questions. He is not only *on the go*, but he is also *in the know*. It is notable that Tychicus is not only relied on to deliver the mail, but he is also trusted to deliver an update on Paul's situation, answer any questions raised by Paul's communication, and to provide further explanation, if needed. As Proverbs says, "Like a snow-cooled drink at harvest time is a trustworthy messenger to the one who sends him; he refreshes the spirit of his master" (25:13). Send the right person, and communication is enhanced. Send the wrong person, and communication may be bungled.

Likely the first public readings of Paul's letters in Ephesus, Colossae, and Crete are not the first times Tychicus hears the contents. He may have been present with Paul when the letters were dictated, and may have assisted Paul by providing feedback on how the words were landing.

In 2 Timothy 4:12, Paul indicates his sending of Tychicus to Ephesus, which would make Timothy free to rejoin Paul in Rome, as the apostle desires (vv. 9, 21). Tychicus must be a loyal and trustworthy man, since he is given such great responsibility. This "dear brother and faithful servant in the Lord" (Ephesians 6:21) comes from Asia Minor and accompanies Paul to Jerusalem with the offering for the poor saints there (Acts 20:4), and he is also with Paul in his last imprisonment (Titus 3:12).

Aristarchus

Aristarchus first appears in Acts 19:29 as a "traveling companion" of Paul who gets caught up in a riot in Ephesus. It may be that Aristarchus is converted when Paul visits the synagogue in Thessalonica during his second missionary journey, then joins Paul in Ephesus during his third missionary journey. In Ephesus, Aristarchus and Gaius—known to be Paul's companions—are seized and manhandled by the angry mob and rushed into the theater when the mob is unable to locate Paul himself. Aristarchus and Gaius are in a precarious position until the city clerk is finally able to persuade the crowd to disperse.

Aristarchus goes on two long journeys with Paul, first through Macedonia (Acts 20:4), and again when Paul sails for Italy (Acts 27:1–2; Colossians 4:10). He is mentioned in two of Paul's letters, described as a "fellow prisoner" (Colossians 4:10) and a "fellow worker" (Philemon 1:24).

Leadership Lesson: **Not every person who offers significant service is prominent and conspicuous.**

Aristarchus is one of many of Paul's colleagues who are not high-profile individuals. Nevertheless, they are held in high regard by Paul and contribute to the apostle's leadership in significant ways. More important than how high the profile is how deep the impact.

John Mark

John Mark first enters Paul's story during Paul's famine-relief visit to Jerusalem with Barnabas. At the end of their time in Jerusalem, they take John Mark back to Antioch. John Mark must have been one of the bright young lights in the Jerusalem church. Barnabas in particular sees in John Mark qualities that can be developed and used in the Christian mission.

John Mark is chosen to accompany Paul and Barnabas on the first missionary journey. Soon into the trip, however, he bails and returns to Jerusalem, perhaps to his mother's house (see Acts 12:12). Maybe he does not have the constitution for the rigors of missionary life. Or maybe he resents Paul taking the leadership reins from Barnabas, or is physically sick or homesick, or is intimidated by what may lie ahead. He returns home, a source of great disappointment and grief to Paul, who sees John Mark's departure as desertion.

Leadership Lesson: There will always be people who leave.

In every church, every ministry, every organization, there are people who, for various reasons, move on to other things. Sometimes they have good reasons—maybe life circumstances necessitate relocation. Sometimes the reasons aren't as good—they lose heart, or nerve, or commitment to the mission. Whatever the reason, be careful not to burn bridges. Your paths may cross again in a way that can bless both you and them.

When Barnabas wants to take John Mark with them on the second missionary trip, Paul refuses, and Paul and Barnabas split over the disagreement. It should be noted that John Mark is also a relative of Barnabas—they are cousins (see Colossians 4:10).

Leadership Lesson: People often deserve a second chance.

Rather than asking, "Does this person deserve a second chance?" perhaps it is better to ask, "Is this the right time for a second chance?" Should a person who abandons a serious responsibility be allowed the opportunity to do so again? Barnabas says absolutely yes. Paul says absolutely no. A. T. Robinson notes, "No one can rightly blame Barnabas for giving his cousin John Mark a second chance, nor Paul for fearing to risk him again. One's judgment may go with Paul, but one's heart goes with Barnabas."[2]

In time, John Mark matures, and Paul mellows. While Paul earlier looks on John Mark with a critical eye, the day will come when Paul includes him in a list of those who have proven "a comfort" to him (Colossians 4:10–11). John Mark has no doubt matured under the wise mentorship of Barnabas and, later, as Peter's assistant. In time, Paul's heart softens toward John Mark, who will reappear as one of Paul's companions in his Ephesian imprisonment. In 2 Timothy 4, Paul requests that Timothy bring John Mark with him to visit Paul in prison, revealing that John Mark has again become a trusted companion (v. 11).

Leadership Lesson: One of the great joys of leadership is to see someone restored after experiencing failure.

It is a wonderful privilege to walk in seasons of recovery and reinstatement with those who have suffered a moral lapse or ministry failure. Organizations, ministries, and churches are to be commended when they provide resources for recovery and restoration and offer the possibility of a second chance after various types of failure.

Questions for Leadership Development

1. Who are the ministry partners with whom God has blessed you?

2. When have you needed a troubleshooter or peacemaker to assist you in the repair of a relationship that has been strained by your leadership?

3. Who helps you ensure that you communicate well?

4. When have you had the opportunity to give someone a second chance?

5. When were you given a second chance, and how did that offer of grace change you?

EIGHT

THIRD-CIRCLE CONNECTIONS: PROVIDENTIAL CONTACTS

I plan to do so when I go to Spain. I hope to see you while passing through and to have you assist me on my journey there, after I have enjoyed your company for a while.
—Romans 15:24

Leaders often experience providential encounters—seemingly serendipitous occasions when you meet the right person at the right time. Because of a fortuitous encounter a situation is diffused, a tragedy averted, or a doorway opens to tremendous possibilities. Paul has many such providential encounters. Ananias, whose story is told in chapter 3, is perhaps the first person with whom Paul has such a meeting, but there will be many, many more.

Lydia

When Paul visits Philippi during the course of his second missionary journey, he deviates from his usual strategy of starting in the synagogue. Instead, he joins a prayer meeting along the riverside, outside the gates of the city (see Acts 16:13). The first gospel sermon in Europe is given that day to the women gathered there, among whom is Lydia, who will be the first documented convert to Christianity in Europe. Then and there, she is baptized in the river by Paul, along with her whole household. She insists that Paul and his whole traveling party—Silas, Timothy, and Luke—stay in her home, which becomes the base of their ministry in Philippi.

Lydia, a businesswoman from Thyatira, is a "dealer in purple cloth" (v. 14). She runs a business selling the rich, indigo-dyed cloth for which Thyatira is famous. Probably a widow, she is a woman of considerable business capacity. Apparently, she has moved to Philippi to expand her business operation. Noble and true-hearted, Lydia becomes a devoted supporter of Paul. After Paul and Silas are set free, following their beating and imprisonment in Philippi, they return to Lydia's house to encourage and refresh the believers there, before departing the city (v. 40).

Leadership Lesson: One way to identify a gifted leader is by the quality of the people around them.

Genuine leaders tend to be surrounded by gifted, capable, effective, devoted people. Such qualities characterize Paul's first convert in Europe. Lydia offers to host him and his traveling companions as an expression of her gratitude, and she is persuasive enough that they finally accept her generous offer of hospitality. In the New Testament, the person of peace is the one who opens the way for the gospel to enter their social group, family, or community. Jesus taught his disciples to search for a worthy person, or person of peace, on entering a village. Throughout the book of Acts, this is played out as the apostles find persons of peace who help them share the gospel. Just as Levi opens his home and invites all his friends to see Jesus in Mark 2, so Lydia's hospitality and influence open the door for Paul to share the gospel with many in Philippi.

Jason

Jason, of Thessalonica, is an early Christian believer mentioned in Acts 17:5–9 and Romans 16:21. He provides lodging for Paul and his traveling companions, and his house becomes a refuge and the base of their operations in that city. While Paul is staying with Jason, some Jews in Thessalonica become jealous of Paul's ministry. Bent on violence, they form a mob and start a riot, hoping to detain Paul. When they cannot locate Paul and Silas at Jason's house, Jason is apprehended and made to assume the financial burden of posting bond before he is released. Paul has to leave quickly and secretly.

Leadership Lesson: The importance of hospitality cannot be overstated.

Both Lydia in Philippi and Jason in Thessalonica respond to the gospel, open their homes to serve as hosts for Paul's ministry team, and may well continue to host their respective churches after Paul leaves the city. The expense of providing hospitality for Paul and his companions comes at significant cost to Jason, who also pays a price in fines and reputation.

Crispus and Sosthenes

Crispus, ruler of the synagogue in Corinth, is mentioned in 1 Corinthians 1:14. He and his household are converted when Paul visits Corinth during his second missionary journey. For several weeks Paul speaks in the synagogue until the unbelieving Jews oppose him and become abusive (Acts 18:5–6). Paul shakes out his clothes before them as an expression of protest. At the invitation of Titius Justus, who owns the house next door to the synagogue, Paul continues his ministry in the city from that location.

The first convert, after Paul relocates from the synagogue to the house, is none other than Crispus, the ruler of the synagogue. When the influential leader surrenders his heart to the Messiah, his whole household also comes to faith, as well as many others from the Corinthian synagogue. Crispus is one of the few people Paul baptizes in Corinth (1 Corinthians 1:14).

Later, Sosthenes, the man who replaces Crispus as leader of the synagogue, attempts to stir up trouble for Paul, but he is sternly rebuffed by the Roman proconsul, Gallio. When the Jews at Corinth are prevented from punishing Paul by Gallio's unwillingness to hear their case, they angrily seize Sosthenes and beat him. When Paul writes his first letter to the Corinthians, Sosthenes is listed as coauthor (1:1), which indicates that he has apparently become a believer in the meantime.

Leadership Lesson: **A leader's impact is strengthened when people of influence join the mission.**

The church in Corinth experiences significant growth, due in part to the conversions of Crispus and Sosthenes, who have significant social standing.

Phoebe

Phoebe is mentioned in Romans 16, where Paul commends her to the Roman believers as a leader ("deacon") of the church in Cenchreae, a seaport about five miles from Corinth. The Romans are asked to receive her into their homes and hearts with a gracious and friendly manner and to provide for any need she may have, just as she has provided for the needs of many others.

The letter to the Romans, which Paul writes from Corinth, closes with Paul's travel plans. Apparently, Phoebe will travel west with the letter to Rome while Paul will travel east with the offering for Jerusalem. N. T. Wright suggests that Phoebe is likely entrusted "with the responsibility of delivering and almost certainly expounding on the letter to the Romans."[1]

Leadership Lesson: The ministry of women is prominent in Paul's leadership.

Phoebe is but one of a larger cohort of women who partner closely with Paul—others include Chloe (1 Corinthians 1:11); Nympha (Colossians 4:15); Apphia (Philemon 2), Euodia and Syntyche (Philippians 4:2–3); and Junia (Romans 16:7). Sometimes Paul gets labeled as anti-women, but Phoebe and her sisters in ministry would surely testify otherwise. Because the Romans are not acquainted with Phoebe, Paul introduces her as his emissary and provides them with Phoebe's credentials. She is a deacon and a leader, and Paul wants the Romans to know it. Part of her calling from God is to lead the church. It is clear she is a trusted member of the body of believers in Cenchreae. Paul likely entrusts Phoebe not only to carry his letter to the Romans but also to explain the letter to its first hearers.

Onesiphorus

Onesiphorus is only mentioned twice in Paul's writings—2 Timothy 1:16–18 and 4:19. Paul indicates that Onesiphorus is helpful to him and is not afraid to be associated with Paul despite his imprisonment. When Onesiphorus comes to Rome, he is diligent to seek out Paul at a time when it may be not only difficult to find the apostle but also dangerous to be recognized as one of his associates. He gives Paul great help in Ephesus, which is evidently Onesiphorus's home city. His help means much to Paul when he needs it most, and Paul appreciates Onesiphorus's courage and determination.

Epaphroditus

Epaphroditus of Philippi is a man whom Paul calls his "fellow soldier" (Philippians 2:25). The members of the Philippian church entrust Epaphroditus to deliver a gift of money to Paul, who will use it to provide for his expenses while he is under house arrest in Rome (see Philippians 4:18). Epaphroditus is also tasked, as a representative of the Philippian church, with giving Paul whatever help he can. While in Rome, Epaphroditus falls ill and nearly dies. News of his illness gets back to Philippi and fills his friends with anxiety. Epaphroditus, though he desires to stay on in Rome and make himself useful to Paul, is also eager to relieve the fears of his friends. Paul sends Epaphroditus back with the letter to the Philippians, in which Paul not only thanks the Philippian believers for their gift but also takes sole responsibility for Epaphroditus's return to them. Paul expresses deep appreciation for what Epaphroditus has done for him already and encourages the Philippians to honor him well.

Agabus

Agabus is a prophet whose first mention is in Acts 11, when he appears at Antioch and predicts an approaching famine that will affect everyone around the world (vv. 27–28). In response to this warning, the believers in Antioch send significant help to the believers in Judea.

Many years later, Agabus meets Paul at Caesarea and warns him of the terrible things that will happen if Paul continues on his journey to Jerusalem (21:10–12). In symbolic action similar to that of the prophet Jeremiah (see Jeremiah 13), Agabus takes Paul's belt, ties up his own hands and feet, and proclaims that Paul will experience the same and be delivered to the custody of the gentiles. When Paul's friends hear the prophecy, they try to discourage him from proceeding, but Paul is resolute. Agabus's prophecy will be fulfilled.

Leadership Lesson: **Sometimes prophetic utterances are unpleasant to hear, but they are communicated both for our own good and the good of others.**

In both instances in which Agabus prophesies, he faithfully delivers the message God has given him and leaves it up to the hearers to make an appropriate response. In the former case, the purpose is to spur the Antioch church to bless the church in Jerusalem. In the latter case, it seems the purpose is to mentally prepare Paul for what will befall him in Jerusalem.

Claudius Lysias

Claudius Lysias is the Roman commander of the Roman garrison in Jerusalem (see Acts 21:31–23:30). When a riot breaks out in the temple area because some Asiatic Jews mistakenly assume Paul is desecrating the temple by bringing a gentile into the courtyard, Lysias quickly responds with his soldiers and succeeds in rescuing Paul from the hands of the mob. Since Paul is the apparent troublemaker, Lysias binds him with two chains and demands to know who he is and the cause of the disturbance. The Roman commander has mistaken Paul for an Egyptian anarchist and Jewish revolutionary. When Paul responds to Lysias in Greek, asking permission to address to the Jewish mob, Lysias realizes his mistake and grants Paul permission.

Paul's speech has no calming effect on the mob. Lysias then determines to learn the truth by scourging Paul, and is quickly dismayed to learn he may have violated the rights of his prisoner, since such punishment is illegal to perpetrate against a Roman citizen. Paul is released from his bonds. Lysias then initiates a different approach, summoning the Sanhedrin to a meeting that ends in an uproar and necessitates conducting Paul back to the safety of the barracks.

That very evening, Lysias learns of a plot to kill Paul, and he dispatches two hundred soldiers, seventy horsemen, and two hundred spearmen to accompany Paul to Caesarea (Acts 23:23–24). He delivers Paul to Felix, along with a letter explaining the circumstances, acknowledging Paul's innocence, and putting Lysias's own actions in the best possible light (vv. 25–30).

Leadership Lesson: Be sensitive to the possibility of providential encounters.

Just as "some people have shown hospitality to angels without knowing it" (Hebrews 13:2), it may be that God has ordained that your path will opportunely cross the path of an individual who will provide an unexpected but needed blessing.

Questions for Leadership Development

1. How might you follow Paul's example and champion the gifts, leadership, and service of women?

2. What role does hospitality play in your organization or ministry?

3. What characteristics are evident in the lives of those you know with the gift of hospitality?

4. Whose influence has been a blessing to you?

5. What providential contacts can you identify?

PART 3

THE LEADER'S CHARACTER

The Inner Qualities that Sustain Leadership

Not only so, but we also glory in our sufferings,
because we know that suffering produces perseverance;
perseverance, character; and character, hope.
—Romans 5:3–4

As an apple tree does not produce apples by Act of Parliament,
but because it is its nature so to do, so the character of Christ
cannot be produced in his people by rules and regulations;
it must be the fruit of his Spirit within them.
—F. F. Bruce, Paul: Apostle of the Heart Set Free

Character is the most important asset of a leader. While a sense of call may be the gateway to the leadership journey, evidence of character provides the passport.

A person of character is a person whose life demonstrates virtue. A list of virtuous character traits could become lengthy. Our exploration of Paul's character will focus on trustworthiness, resilience, compassion, self-control, and humility. These character traits appear repeatedly across the spectrum of leadership positions, notably among leaders who faithfully toil in less prominent venues. The character of such leaders may go unrecognized and unsung, but it is not unimportant.

Leadership Lesson: **Leadership is not about charisma or technique as much as it is about character.**

Skill is not the first thing that qualifies leaders; character is. While one can observe many different styles of leadership, what matters most is the substance—character. Leaders can lead only to a point if they rely solely on personality or performance. In order to lead well and far, a leader must have character. Work twice as hard on your character as you do on your competence.

For Christian leaders, character is the result of the work of the Spirit in our lives. When we give ourselves completely to God, the Holy Spirit is free to work within us, producing the character of Christ. Paul's description of the fruit of the Spirit is a portrayal of the character of Christ: love, joy, peace, patience, kindness, goodness, faithfulness, gentleness, self-control (Galatians 5:22–23). The world hungers for this sweet fruit.

Leadership Lesson: **While competence may determine a leader's breadth, character determines a leader's depth.**

It is possible to have a wide array of talents and abilities yet be shallow in character. One will never have enough ability if character is lacking. If the leader takes care of the depth, God will take care of the breadth. When I meet with church leadership teams and pastors, I often ask lay leaders to describe their pastor's gifts. In response, some identify competencies while others describe character. While the former tend to speak with appreciation, the latter speak with deep admiration. Of the two, character is of primary importance. Competence is a matter of deliberate practice. A leader of character recognizes the duty to be competent and has the self-discipline to submit to the required deliberate practice.

NINE

TRUSTWORTHY

Now it is required that those who have been given a trust must prove faithful.
—1 Corinthians 4:2

Trustworthiness—the confidence others have in you because of your ability to be truthful and loyal—is a fitting place to begin our consideration of Paul's character. The strength of a leader's character is largely dependent on the trustworthiness of that leader. Paul, writing to Timothy, references the link between trustworthiness and the mission: "I thank Christ Jesus our Lord, who has given me strength, that he considered me trustworthy, appointing me to his service" (1 Timothy 1:12). Paul makes the same link when writing to the Corinthians: "I am simply discharging the trust committed to me" (1 Corinthians 9:17b). The mission given to Paul—apostle to the gentiles—is not an easy assignment, but the strength of Paul's character will enable him to fulfill his mission and prove his trustworthiness.

Integrity

Integrity is the quality of being honest and authentic, of keeping your word, and of living in accordance with your deeply held values. Integrity is present when your actions are in sync with the values you espouse. It is critical that the leader's personal values align with the values of the organization or ministry the leader serves—or else it becomes difficult, if not impossible, to maintain integrity. Integrity involves living in accordance with strong moral and ethical principles. It is the quality of inner resonance. Integrity—a life lived with credibility, loyalty, and authenticity—is the primary quality on which healthy relationships are built. Leaders with integrity are worthy of the confidence others place in them because they earn it with honorable service.

Leadership Lesson: **Most organizations expect their leaders to display strong morals and high character, and live lives marked by integrity.**

This expectation is certainly not limited to ministry-related organizations. One instance of a lack of integrity—a moral lapse—can have employment consequences in most organizations, even if the moral lapse occurs outside the work environment. Unfortunately, leaders' moral failures make news headlines, while the consistent moral integrity that is displayed daily by many other leaders goes unnoticed and unremarked.

Dissonance occurs when a leader's mission and message do not match up with that leader's behavior. Such dissonance can be evidence of the lack of integrity that often disqualifies leaders—not just leaders of churches and ministry-related organizations but in all spheres of leadership.

There is no dissonance between Paul's public life and his private life. His words match his actions. His conduct aligns with his commission. Paul communicates the importance of integrity to two young leaders he is mentoring. Timothy is told, "Now the overseer is to be above reproach, faithful to his wife, temperate, self-controlled, respectable, hospitable, able to teach, not given to drunkenness, not violent but gentle, not quarrelsome, not a lover of money.

. . . He must also have a good reputation with outsiders, so that he will not fall into disgrace and into the devil's trap" (1 Timothy 3:2–3, 7). Titus is similarly encouraged: "Since an overseer manages God's household, he must be blameless—not overbearing, not quick-tempered, not given to drunkenness, not violent, nor pursuing dishonest gain. Rather, he must be hospitable, one who loves what is good, who is self-controlled, upright, holy and disciplined" (Titus 1:7–8).

Paul's integrity is clearly seen when he and Barnabas are in Lystra in Acts 14. They encounter a man there who has been disabled since birth—he has never walked. When Paul heals the man, the crowd begins to hail Paul and Barnabas as gods. They call Barnabas Zeus, and Paul is called Hermes. When the crowd wants to offer sacrifices to the two missionaries, Paul and Barnabas tear their clothes in protest and hurry to stop them, assuring the crowd they are just men and pointing them to the true, living God. They refuse to receive any kind of tribute that is not due them, and they will not see the crowd misled, even in a way that would greatly benefit them. Their actions are a true sign of humility, and a contrast from Herod's acceptance of praise as a god, which ends in his death (see Acts 12:19–24).

Integrity matters.

Leadership Lesson: Great leaders demonstrate integrity.

There is no deception, no guile, no manipulation in their leadership. They do not have divided hearts. There is no attempt to deceive by speaking one thing but believing another, or of communicating something you know not to be true. The lives of leaders with integrity are marked by authenticity and genuineness. Such leaders have a reputation for unimpeachable integrity. They are upright, sound in character, and absent any serious moral blemish. The presence of such integrity in the life of the leader makes it easy for loyalty to be cultivated in the culture of the organization. The level of an organization's confidence in a leader rises in proportion to the level of the leader's trustworthiness. The longer trustworthiness is demonstrated, the deeper the confidence of the organization in the character of the leader.

Faithfulness

A second component of trustworthiness is faithfulness. Faithfulness is a steadfast, unfailing commitment that results in dependability and reliability. There are two general areas in which the absence of faithfulness is most often exposed in leaders. The first occurs when leaders become unfaithful to their calling by sacrificing the mission in times of difficulty—they quit. The second occurs when leaders become unfaithful to their calling by sacrificing character in times of distraction—they sin. Such distractions are often linked to inappropriate indulgences or peccadillos and are often preceded by a sense of entitlement. Paul is able to avoid both the temptation to sacrifice the mission and the temptation to sacrifice character. His faithfulness to the mission is exemplary, and it is due in large part to his single-minded desire to please God.

Obstacles and adversity are the anvil on which faithfulness is shaped and tested. The challenges of setback, loss, failure, disappointment, and defeat do not indicate a lack of character. Rather, they provide the conditions in which character is forged and displayed. Leadership can be difficult. It can be a grind. It often is for Paul. Willingness to stay engaged with the mission, despite difficulties and distractions, proves one's trustworthiness. Trustworthiness is established by faithfulness.

Leadership Lesson: Faithfulness is proven over the long haul.

Doing what you said you were going to do when you said you were going to do it will set you apart from less dependable leaders. Toward the end of Paul's ministry, he writes what is likely his last letter—the second letter to Timothy. In that letter, Paul testifies, "I have fought the good fight, I have finished the race, I have kept the faith" (4:7). May each of us be able to proclaim the same when our leadership journey nears completion.

Accountability

A third component of trustworthiness is accountability. While Paul's primary accountability is to God (see 1 Thessalonians 2:4–6), there is also accountability evident in his human relationships. Accountability is the willingness both to accept responsibility and be answerable for that responsibility. While accountability does not guarantee trustworthiness, it does create a climate in which trustworthiness can flourish.

Leadership Lesson: **One reason governing boards and leadership teams are important is for the accountability they can provide a leader.**

Some leadership opportunities have significant, intentional, built-in accountability. Other opportunities can easily provide an escape from accountability unless leaders are careful to build it in. Accountability is especially important in start-up situations, when policies and structures have not yet been fully developed. Having a governing board or leadership team in place early, with an awareness of the importance of requiring accountability of the new leader and building accountability into the DNA of the organization, can help ensure long-term health and effectiveness.

We will discuss just three of the many ways Paul's accountability is evident. First, Paul demonstrates accountability in the raising of an offering for the church in Jerusalem (1 Corinthians 16:1–4; 2 Corinthians 8:1–9:15; Romans 15:14–32). Paul has a sense of delicacy where money is concerned and is careful to model financial integrity. Though he raises the funds, he is careful to avoid impropriety and insists that others deliver the funds to Jerusalem.

Second, the reports Paul provides to the church in Antioch after his first and second missionary journeys provide a means of accountability (Acts 14:26–28; 18:22–23). He is careful to inform the sending church of his progress in the effort to evangelize the gentiles. Leaders do well to regularly report on their progress toward achieving the mission. Such reports often include an accounting of the effectiveness of the mission, challenges encountered and how those challenges have been addressed, and how resources have been invested in the mission.

Third, the presence of traveling companions and ministry colleagues provides ever-present accountability for Paul's actions and his attitudes. Paul does not lead in isolation. His life is lived with a group of coworkers who observe his leadership daily. These relationships, marked by transparency and authenticity, become a network of accountability that serves Paul well.

Questions for Leadership Development

1. Are the failings of leaders usually due to a lack of character or a lack of competence?

2. How does a leader develop trustworthiness?

3. To what degree is accountability present in your current leadership responsibility? How might you intentionally strengthen your commitment to accountability?

4. Which temptation is most prevalent in your life—the temptation to sacrifice the mission (to quit) or the temptation to sacrifice character (to sin)?

5. What do 1 Timothy 3:1–7 and Titus 1:6–9 say about the importance of character?

6. What makes you a leader God can trust?

— TEN —

RESILIENT

*Therefore we do not lose heart. Though outwardly
we are wasting away, yet inwardly we are
being renewed day by day.*
—2 Corinthians 4:16

Paul's ministry faces stiff resistance, extreme hardship, even violence. More than any other apostle, he is exposed to suffering and distress. His resilience enables him to bounce back from these difficulties. Resilience is the capacity to adapt and recover in the face of adversity, trauma, and significant sources of stress. This character trait allows leaders to maintain effective engagement with the mission despite significant adversity. Character is often *developed* during adversity, but it is also always *revealed* during adversity.

Perseverance is a component of resilience. Perseverance is the ability to not give up; resilience is the ability to continually recover while not giving up. You can display perseverance without resilience; you cannot display resilience without perseverance. Perseverance allows leaders to last; resilience allows leaders to last *well*.

Paul, speaking from experience, warns Timothy that difficult times will come (see 2 Timothy 3:1). In these times, resilience allows a leader to continue to serve effectively. Resilience is *courageous endurance*—courage in the face of suffering, endurance in the face of hardship. Amid the trials and tribulations of his ministry, Paul demonstrates both.

Courage in the Face of Suffering

Suffering is Paul's constant companion over the course of his service as a Christian leader. He becomes a long-suffering leader, not only in the sense of patience (which is how the term is usually used) but also in the sense that he displays persevering grit in the face of prolonged distress.

The story of Paul's call includes a dark and significant forecast. A sign of Paul's approaching troubles is given early in the story of his summons to Christian leadership. The words the Lord speaks to Ananias regarding Paul—"I will show him how much he must suffer for my name" (Acts 9:16)—make plain that suffering will be Paul's lot. And suffer Paul does. The magnitude and variety of the hardships he endures in the course of his ministry are daunting, as seen in this passage written to the Corinthians:

> Five times I received from the Jews the forty lashes minus one. Three times I was beaten with rods, once I was pelted with stones, three times I was shipwrecked, I spent a night and a day in the open sea, I have been constantly on the move. I have been in danger from rivers, in danger from bandits, in danger from my fellow Jews, in danger from Gentiles; in danger in the city, in danger in the country, in danger at sea; and in danger from false believers. I have labored and toiled and have often gone without sleep; I have known hunger and thirst and have often gone without food; I have been cold and naked.
> (2 Corinthians 11:24–27)

Paul endures great anguish and suffering. He is pressed, perplexed, and pursued. He suffers sleeplessness, hunger, physical violence, imprisonment, toil, temptation, and pressure. He comes near death again and again. Yet he remains resolute, courageous, un-

daunted, indomitable, determined, tough, and tenacious. His fortitude is amazing. Paul is resilient.

Paul speaks of having on five occasions "received from the hands
of the Jews the forty lashes minus one." These beatings probably
occur as Paul submits to synagogue discipline. Such chastisement
would begin with a trial by the elders. Thirty-nine lashes is the
maximum amount before the punishment is considered cruel or in-
humane, so Paul is saying he received the maximum punishment
five times. Synagogue scourging is regarded as correction—purging
the offense so that the offender might resume their place in the synagogue. The punishment is designed to be painful enough to keep
the guilty party from repeating the offense without being life-en-
dangering.

Jewish floggings are significantly different from Roman floggings. Both might be meted out with whips or birch rods, but Roman floggings could kill a man, whereas Jewish floggings are the
official punishment of the synagogue, designed to provide stern
correction, rather than humiliation. Paul would be stripped to the
waist and either bound between two pillars or bent over a waist-high
whipping pillar, his back well exposed to the lictor. The whip would
be long enough to curl round the shoulder and cover the chest or
back, depending on how the offender is turned. Whips could con-
tain a single lash (inflicted thirty-nine times), three lashes (inflicted
thirteen times), or thirteen lashes (inflicted three times). Paul receives 195 stripes over the course of his ministry. He is physically
and emotionally marked for life.

Expulsion from the synagogue, or from the city, always includes
flogging: "Here's a good reason to not come back here." Nowhere in
Acts is there mention of Paul's receiving stripes from a synagogue. It
is striking that Luke does not mention any of the five lashings. It may
be that some (or all) are received at the synagogue in Tarsus before
Barnabas summons Paul to Antioch and the missionary trips begin.

Leadership Lesson: A Christian leader must be willing to endure suffering—both physical and emotional—for Christ.

Intense suffering will mark Paul's ministry. Rather than resent these sufferings, Paul rejoices in them because they build character and enable him to share in Christ's sufferings (see Romans 5:3; Philippians 3:10; Colossians 1:24). He gladly accepts his share in the sufferings of Christ and readily endures injuries and trials. For a leader, suffering is to be seen as essential to one's development. One highly effective leader I know believes that leaders *only* develop through suffering.[1] Hardship isn't just something that leaders endure; it is the soil in which leaders grow. Perhaps this is why real leaders demonstrate true compassion, allowing them to demand much from people (and ignite their growth) when others would attempt to pamper them (and unintentionally hinder them). The religious establishment—who stand to benefit the most from the status quo—are vicious in punishing Paul for deviating from their protocols. Often the most likely people to punish an innovative leader are other leaders who are threatened by a message that requires significant change.[2]

One of the three times Paul is beaten with rods occurs in Philippi, when he and Silas suffer a severe beating before being thrown into prison (see Acts 16). When the magistrates find out that Paul is a Roman citizen, they are fearful. When the magistrates order the jailer to release Paul and Silas, Paul replies, "They beat us publicly without a trial, even though we are Roman citizens, and threw us into prison. And now do they want to get rid of us quietly? No! Let them come themselves and escort us out" (v. 37). The magistrates personally acknowledge their error and request that Paul and Silas depart the city.

At Lystra, Paul experiences one of the most terrifying episodes of his ministry (see Acts 14:8–20). After healing a man who couldn't walk, Paul and Barnabas are mistaken for the gods Hermes and

Zeus. Then antagonists from Pisidian Antioch and Iconium—probably traveling merchants who just happen to be in the neighborhood—stir up the crowd against Paul and Barnabas. The stoning begins. Bloodied and broken, Paul is dragged out of the city and left for dead. Likely in excruciating pain, he gets up, wipes the blood off his face, and struggles to make his way back into the city. The next day Paul and Barnabas leave town, and the battered Paul finds respite in Derbe, where he recuperates during the winter.

Leadership Lesson: Finding a purpose in suffering is imperative for resilience.

When it comes to extreme suffering, few know more about it than Viktor Frankl, who survived the Nazi death camps. David Brooks writes, "Frankl argued that we often can't control what happens to us in life, that we can control only how we respond to it. If we respond to terrible circumstances with tenacity, courage, unselfishness, and dignity, then we can add a deeper meaning to life. One can win small daily victories over hard circumstances. Frankl liked to paraphrase Nietzsche: 'He who has a why to live for can bear with almost any how.'" Brooks continues, "Suffering can make people self-centered, loveless, humorless, and angry. But we all know cases where suffering didn't break people but broke them open—made them more caring toward and knowledgeable about the suffering of others. And the old saying that we suffer our way to wisdom is not wrong. We often learn more from the hard times than the happy ones."[3] For Paul, to endure hardship is to identify with Christ. One gets the sense that Paul never feels closer to Christ than when he is suffering for Christ. Paul also recognizes the role suffering plays in development (see Romans 5:3–4). Charles Swindoll notes, "The crucible of pain and hardship is God's schoolroom where Christians learn humility, compassion, character, patience, and grace."[4] In addition to developing character, suffering can also serve as a gateway to empathy. The experience of pain can allow leaders to comfort others more effectively. Suffering can play a beneficial role in a leader's life.

Physical suffering can be brought on by painful accidents, illness, or the brutal actions of others. Emotional suffering can be brought on by deep concern *for* others or by deep rejection *by* others. Paul is intimately familiar with both. There is ample evidence that Paul experiences significant emotional distress. In 2 Corinthians, he speaks of bearing emotional burdens: "Besides everything else, I face daily the pressure of my concern for all the churches" (11:28). Traumatic events, relationship difficulties, and his deep care for people facing significant threats could easily lead to depression, anxiety, and sleeplessness.

Leadership Lesson: Leaders often carry the scars of suffering.

Paul outwardly carries the scars from his imprisonments, severe beatings, stoning, shipwrecks, near drowning, and ambushes. He also inwardly carries the marks of his emotional distress: insomnia, loneliness, anxiety, depression. These marks, while often not visible to others, manifest themselves in stress-related illnesses and challenges to mental health. Many of the best leaders I know—local church pastors—often bear burdens unknown to others. Because of the importance of keeping a confidence, they bear in silence the burdens of those for whom they care, often in ways known only to God. Some of those burdens include the painful disintegration of relationships, providing end-of-life care, concern over wayward children, and the distress of debilitating illness.

Endurance in the Face of Hardship

In addition to suffering from beatings, flogging, and stoning, Paul faces numerous other hardships, including shipwrecks, constant danger, sleeplessness, hunger, thirst, and frequent imprisonments.

He will write to the Corinthians of a particularly difficult season, "We were harassed at every turn" (2 Corinthians 7:5).

Paul experiences imprisonment in Philippi, Ephesus, Caesarea, and Rome. He writes the prison epistles while captive. Prisons in Paul's day are not usually places of punishment but places where people awaiting trial are remanded. Little effort is made to care for prisoners, who are expected to provide for their own physical needs while incarcerated. The great difficulty with imprisonment is isolation—being cut off from others.

Leadership Lesson: Every leader who is faithful to Christ will share in his suffering.

The true leader must be willing to endure hardship as "a good soldier of Christ Jesus" (2 Timothy 2:3). A challenge often given to ministers being ordained comes from Paul's words to Timothy: "Preach the word; be prepared in season and out of season; correct, rebuke and encourage—with great patience and careful instruction. . . . But you, keep your head in all situations, endure hardship, do the work of an evangelist, discharge all the duties of your ministry" (2 Timothy 4:2, 5).

In 2 Corinthians 1, Paul tells the Corinthians of his trouble in Asia, how he "despaired of life itself" and experienced pressure far beyond his ability to endure. But he also quickly testifies of God's deliverance "from such a deadly peril" and his confidence that God can be trusted to deliver him again (vv. 8–10). God sustains him and brings him through the difficulty.

John MacArthur suggests that a leader must "find strength to endure every kind of trial—including pressure, perplexity, persecution, and pain."[5] Paul speaks of those very trials in a series of four vivid contrasts: "We are hard pressed on every side, but not crushed; perplexed, but not in despair; persecuted, but not abandoned; struck down, but not destroyed" (2 Corinthians 4:8–9). Despite Paul's significant hardships, he gives this testimony of God's deliverance: "You, however, know all about my teaching, my way of life, my purpose, faith, patience, love, endurance, persecutions, sufferings— what kinds of things happened to me in Antioch, Iconium and Lystra, the persecutions I endured. Yet the Lord rescued me from all of them" (2 Timothy 3:10–11).

Leadership Lesson: God's grace is sufficient.

You can trust God in times of great suffering and hardship. Not only is God with you; God will also deliver you. Paul affirms that God has delivered, God is delivering, and God will deliver. God's grace is sufficient.

Paul is tenacious. He has the fortitude that allows a leader to sustain physical difficulty, heartbreak, sorrow, and intense anguish without giving up. Though arrested, persecuted, beaten, imprisoned, and shipwrecked, Paul presses on, refusing to quit. He presses on, despite dangers known as well as suspected. Notwithstanding an abundance of hardship and suffering, Paul *does not quit.* He is resilient. That is character. In a letter to a friend, Abigail Adams observes, "Affliction is the good man's shining time."[6] Paul's courage, character, and resilience shine brightly in the face of affliction.

Before his last journey to Jerusalem, with offerings from the gentile churches, Paul foresees that this visit to Jerusalem will be fraught with danger. At the ports along the way, he is warned by prophetic announcements made by believers that persecution and prison await him if he continues. Still, he continues.

Leadership Lesson: **Leadership is not for the faint at heart.**

Paul's courage is based not so much on his own bravery as on an awareness of the presence of Jesus with him. There are times—notably at Corinth, again in Jerusalem—when Paul is dismayed at the turn of events and has a vision of the Lord Jesus standing right beside him, saying, "Take courage! As you have testified about me in Jerusalem, so you must also testify in Rome" (Acts 23:11). The strength behind Paul's resilience is Jesus's presence and power at work in him.

Questions for Leadership Development

1. Do others tend to be inspired by your faith or discouraged by your fears?

2. What is your typical response when facing adversity?

3. How does your organization or ministry support its leaders?

4. What adversity are you presently facing?

5. What kinds of suffering have you experienced in the past that makes Paul's trials feel relatable to you? Where have you found encouragement to keep going?

— ELEVEN —

COMPASSIONATE

Praise be to the God and Father of our Lord Jesus Christ,
the Father of compassion and the God of all comfort, who
comforts us in all our troubles, so that we can comfort those
in any trouble with the comfort we ourselves receive from
God.
—2 Corinthians 1:3–4

Compassion is more than simply being nice. Compassion involves the giving of oneself with kindness and tender affection in ways that bring comfort to "those in any trouble." This deep caring always results in action. Paul's nature is warm-hearted and fervent, and he is filled with both passion and compassion. Paul cares deeply about people.

Leadership Lesson: **The leaders who most inspire us are the leaders who care about us.**

In our day, a helpful benchmark for evaluating leaders is the degree of compassion they reveal in relationships, especially in challenging, turbulent relationships. Other leadership gifts—vision, charisma, communication—count for little if a leader lacks compassion. Leaders who care about those they serve often discover that their compassion has become contagious. If a leader lives a life of compassion, others will follow suit.

Caring for the Needy

Paul seems to have three guiding passions: first, Jesus is Lord; second, there is no longer Jew or Greek; third, remember the poor. The most obvious evidence of Paul's concern for the needy is in the offerings he collects for the Jerusalem church.

While Paul is in Antioch the church there is visited by Agabus, a prophet from the Jerusalem church. Agabus gives a solemn warning of a famine that will result in a scarcity of food. The church at Antioch receives this revelation and determines to send relief to Jerusalem, which will be hard hit by the drought (see Acts 11:27–30). The Antioch believers know the Jerusalem believers will not be able to afford the high price of food in famine conditions without aid. Paul is interested in this effort—he has strong concern and is eager to see the connection between the two churches strengthened. He and Barnabas are designated to take the offering to Jerusalem.

In Acts 15, after their first missionary journey, Paul and Barnabas meet with the leaders of the Jerusalem church, and the decision is made not to require circumcision of gentile believers. It is agreed that Paul and Barnabas will continue with the evangelism to the gentiles while the Jerusalem church will concentrate their missionary activity toward Jews. The Jerusalem church adds a special request that Barnabas and Paul should "continue to remember the poor" (Galatians 2:10)—a request best understood against the background of the famine relief the church at Antioch previously sent to Jerusalem with Barnabas and Paul. Paul seems to especially take this to heart. He will continue to make famine relief a priority, and remembering the poor will be a hallmark of his ministry. Paul's concern for the poor is especially evident in 2 Corinthians 8–9 and Romans 15.

Leadership Lesson: Generosity is a hallmark of following Jesus.

Paul will write lengthy passages about generous compassion to the Corinthians and the Romans. Compassion for the less fortunate has been a defining characteristic of Christian ministry from the beginning. Because of the generosity and compassion of followers of Jesus, much has been done to alleviate the distress of the poor and needy around the world. Despite all that has been done, much more remains!

The organizing of financial relief from gentile Christians to the Jerusalem church is a major concern of Paul's. He is greatly engaged with the completion of the contributions to the Jerusalem fund made by the churches in Macedonia and Achaia.

Paul instructs the converts at Corinth, suggesting that each household set aside a portion of their income week by week for a year so the church's contribution will be ready to take to Jerusalem the spring of the following year, taken by delegates appointed by the church for that purpose. Paul pays the Macedonian churches—who are themselves likely as needy as the Jerusalem church—great tribute in 2 Corinthians 8 and 9. The Corinthians are encouraged to give out of their comparative affluence as the Macedonians have given from their destitution.

Leadership Lesson: Compassionate ministry is most effective when groups (often churches) collaborate together to address a need.

Compassionate people often respond when three elements are present: first, they are made aware of a need; second, they are given the opportunity to respond in a way that alleviates the need; and third, they have confidence that the resources will be used for the intended purpose.

All three elements are present in Paul's raising of an offering for the Jerusalem church.

In Acts 21, Paul returns to Jerusalem at the conclusion of his third missionary journey. He brings a collection of money from the gentile churches all over Asia to present to the church at Jerusalem because their need is so great. N. T. Wright observes that Paul "realized just how poor the Jerusalem church had become, and he imagined to himself what an impact it would have if the churches of which Jerusalem had been suspicious—those communities that were allowing gentiles into full membership without circumcision—were to band together and send real and lasting help."[1]

The Jerusalem offering has a threefold purpose—first, relief of the saints in Jerusalem, especially the sick, the poor, and the hungry; second, to remind the predominantly gentile churches of their obligation to the Jewish people in general and the Jerusalem church in particular; and third, to communicate to the Jerusalem church the solidarity of the gentile churches. The gentile believers are communicating that they are the same family, the same body. Paul regards his coming to Jerusalem with the offering as an opportunity to show his own people his love for them. He puts on hold his plans to do pioneer missionary work in Spain in order to deliver the compassionate offering to the believers in Jerusalem (see Romans 15:23–29).

The Jerusalem relief fund is designed not only to bring relief to the Christians in Jerusalem, but it is also intended to strengthen the solidarity between gentile and Jewish Christianity. It will also dispel any suspicions the Jerusalem church has about Paul and his mission, and the gentile converts. F. F. Bruce notes that the offering is not just of money: "The gentile delegates were to bring their offerings to Jerusalem, but the gentile delegates themselves were Paul's own offering, presented not so much to the mother-church as to the Lord who, many years before, called Paul to be his apostle to the gentiles."[2]

Compassion for the Marginalized

Paul is an includer. He has great empathy for those who are marginalized or excluded, including those deemed "weaker" in conscience. While Paul has "a robust and emancipated conscience,"[3] he also has warm sympathy for those with more tender sensibilities and concern for their emotional well-being. He will go to great lengths of self-denial for his weaker brethren when it comes to matters such as food restrictions and the observance of special days on which Christians do not see eye to eye. Bruce summarizes Paul's position thus: "Those who have no scruples in such matters should not despise those who have; and those who have scruples should not sit in judgment on those who have none."[4] In Paul's words, "One person considers one day more sacred than another; another considers every day alike. Each of them should be fully convinced in their own mind" (Romans 14:5). He calls for special gentleness and consideration for fellow Christians who are weak in the faith and unemancipated in conscience.

Leadership Lesson: **Strong leaders are empathetic.**

Empathy is the ability to identify with another person so much that you feel what they feel. This aspect of compassion is essential to understanding the essence of one's need and providing comfort. Paul's empathy extends beyond individuals to include groups of believers.

Paul is not detached from the concerns of the poor and powerless. He preaches and models good news to what Jesus called "the least of these" in Matthew 25—the poor, the marginalized, the disadvantaged, and the vulnerable. The presence of the marginalized in Paul's ministry becomes evident by looking at poverty in Paul's churches, the involvement of both enslaved and free persons in the community, and the role of women in Paul's ministry. Like Jesus, Paul cares deeply for people at the margins. He cares for the poor, serves the least in his mission, and models his ministry after Christ, leading a life of compassion, kindness, and care.

Paul encourages the churches he plants to lift up those on the fringes, the oppressed, and the weak. His call to honor the most vulnerable is a call for unity, which he emphasizes in an exhortation to the Corinthian church: "Brothers and sisters, think of what you were when you were called. Not many of you were wise by human standards; not many were influential; not many were of noble birth. But God chose the foolish things of the world to shame the wise; God chose the weak things of the world to shame the strong. God chose the lowly things of this world and the despised things—and the things that are not—to nullify the things that are, so that no one may boast before him" (1 Corinthians 1:26–29).

Leadership Lesson: **Marginality is a circumstance to be overcome through the power of the gospel and the compassion of the followers of Jesus.**

Wealth and social importance are not forbidden, but neither are they signs of superiority. Blessings are to be stewarded with a great sense of responsibility. God's provisions of abundance and opportunity are provided so the beneficiary may be a blessing to others.

Caring for the Sick

Paul's concern for the physical well-being of others and his compassion for the sick is primarily seen in two ways: his healing ministry and his expressed concern and calls for prayer for those who are ill.

According to Acts 14, Paul's first miraculous healing is of a lame man in Lystra, which is similar to Peter's first healing in Acts 3. In both cases, a man who had been lame since birth is immediately cured by being commanded to stand and walk. Other instances of Paul's healing ministry include the healing of a demon-possessed woman in Philippi (16:16–18), the use of Paul's handkerchiefs and aprons as instruments of healing in Ephesus (19:11–12), and the restoration of life to Eutychus in Troas (20:7–12). While shipwrecked on Malta, Paul heals the father of Publius, who is sick in bed suffering from fever and dysentery. All on the island who are sick are subsequently healed (28:7–9). Paul also shares his concern for his acquaintances who are ill, including Timothy (1 Timothy 5:23), Trophimus (2 Timothy 4:20), and Epaphroditus (Philippians 2:25–30).

In spite of Paul's toughness and tenacity, he has a heart of compassion. He also encourages others to show compassion, writing to the church at Colossae, "Therefore, as God's chosen people, holy and dearly loved, clothe yourselves with compassion, kindness, humility, gentleness and patience" (Colossians 3:12). A similar message is included in his letter to the church of Philippi: "Therefore if you have any encouragement from being united with Christ, if any comfort from his love, if any common sharing in the Spirit, if any tenderness and compassion, then make my joy complete by being like-minded, having the same love, being one in spirit and of one mind" (Philippians 2:1–2).

Compassionate leaders realize that God comforts us in our troubles so we can comfort others who are in trouble. Compassionate leaders lead with their hearts.

Questions for Leadership Development

1. Whose compassion for others has been inspiring to you?

2. On a 1–10 scale, how would you rate your commitment to compassion?

3. What can leaders do to respond to those with financial needs?

4. How have you been involved in compassionate endeavors that required the collaboration of multiple groups?

5. What can leaders do to respond to those who are alienated from community?

6. Have you had opportunities to respond to those who are sick or in physical need? If so, what has been your response?

TWELVE

SELF-CONTROLLED

But the fruit of the Spirit is love, joy, peace, forbearance,
kindness, goodness, faithfulness, gentleness and self-control.
Against such things there is no law.
—Galatians 5:22–23

Self-control is the ability to manage one's own emotions and regulate one's responses, and it is an important component of character. It is the capacity to restrain oneself from unhealthy impulses, desires, and behaviors. Many things are beyond our control. We cannot stop the tide from going in or out. Nor can we control the weather with all its extremes. We also have little control over other people—even in our families. We learn to accept, adjust, and adapt our expectations accordingly. We do, however, have the ability (and responsibility) for *self*-control. Perhaps the supreme irony is realizing how little control we sometimes exercise with that over which we have complete control—the self.

Leadership Lesson: One of the primary responsibilities of leadership is accepting responsibility for self-control.

Perhaps the greatest challenge to those in positions of leadership comes in the form of personal discipline—channeling one's own passions in healthy and helpful ways and not allowing desires unbridled freedom.

The first obstacle to leadership success is usually the obstacle of self. Self-control keeps leaders from sabotaging their own effectiveness.

Self-control is the ninth and final fruit of the Spirit listed by Paul in Galatians 5. Though it is listed last, there should be no doubt as to its importance. It is clearly an indispensable attribute for leadership, for without it, leaders continually capitulate to the persistent tug of unhealthy desires as well as sinful temptations.

It is important to understand that self-control is a work of the Holy Spirit, not just the individual. Self-control, according to Paul, is a product of the Holy Spirit's work in our lives. The indwelling presence of the Holy Spirit gives Christian leaders the power and ability to exercise self-control and not be mastered by sinful cravings. Paul writes, "For the Spirit God gave us does not make us timid, but gives us power, love and self-discipline" (2 Timothy 1:7). Christian leaders are controlled not by the sinful nature but by the Holy Spirit (see Romans 8:9), who helps us in our weakness, empowering us to say no to sin.

Leadership Lesson: It is the work of the Spirit within the heart and life of a leader that enables self-control to emerge and flourish.

Self-control is absolutely vital to lasting success in any endeavor in life, but it is often in short supply. Greater self-control becomes possible when the Holy Spirit produces it in the life of a leader. Like all fruit, self-control can flourish if it is nurtured and cultivated. Those whom God calls to lead are those whom God calls to follow the Holy Spirit the most closely.

In 1 Corinthians 9, Paul strongly exhorts us to self-control: "Do you not know that in a race all the runners run, but only one gets the prize? Run in such a way as to get the prize. Everyone who competes in the games goes into strict training. They do it to get a crown that will not last, but we do it to get a crown that will last forever. Therefore I do not run like someone running aimlessly; I do not fight like a boxer beating the air. No, I strike a blow to my body and make it my slave so that after I have preached to others, I myself will not be disqualified for the prize" (vv. 24–27). Because the Corinthians are familiar with the rigors of athletic training, especially in preparation for the Olympic games, Paul likens living a disciplined life to an athlete in training. He does not want to disqualify himself from the race due to a lack of self-control. So, like an Olympic athlete with a strict training regime, Paul disciplines himself, bringing his own body into subjection. He is saying that his body is under his dominion and control, not the other way around. Paul is showing us how self-control is needed to win the race that is before us and to live the life that is "holy and pleasing to God" (see Romans 12:1). Self-control teaches us to say no to lesser desires in order to say yes to nobler purposes and higher principles. Saying no puts us in charge of our appetites, rather than our appetites exercising control over us.

Leadership Lesson: The body is a good servant but a bad master.

For our own good and God's glory, we bring the appetites and desires of our own body under control. The indulgences we grant our appetites, the satisfactions we seek for our needs, and the activities we engage in—all reveal the degree to which we reflect the virtue of self-control. Perhaps in the same way a coach helps an athlete reach their full potential, the use of a leadership coach might help some leaders cooperate more completely with the Holy Spirit in developing self-control to reach their full potential.

The discipline of an athlete is mostly their own responsibility. Every serious athlete keeps their body under control. Many other people, by contrast, are controlled *by* their bodies. Athletes have a training regimen, a nutrition regimen, and a sleep and rest regimen. The athlete's body is nourished to stay healthy, exercised to stay fit, worked to build muscle, and rested for proper recovery. Attention to detail is employed for peak performance. Paul says the victorious runner is an example of rigorous self-control (1 Corinthians 9:25). It is a matter of concentrating not only while he is racing but also in all other areas of life because his whole life impacts the race. The runner religiously follows a robust program within a rigid schedule: rising at a certain time, eating certain foods at certain intervals, exercising a certain way, sleeping at a certain time. Avoiding indulgences, runners must also abstain from many perfectly legitimate things that simply do not fit into the program. Accountability, maintained by a fellow athlete or a coach, may also be necessary where self-control is deficient.

Leadership Lesson; Leaders can become disqualified due to a lack of self-control.

If we let our desires determine our decisions, our lives can quickly spin out of control. Self-control is a discipline that God grows in us when we continually allow the Holy Spirit to shape our character and direct our lives. Of course, the importance of self-control is not just limited to the physical realm but also applies to the tongue, to time, and to the mind. One relatively recent, unfortunate development is the trend in leadership toward fewer behaviors being disqualifying. The prevailing mood in much of society is that no one is ever really disqualified from leadership. Often a disgraced leader is restored immediately if they make a public display of remorse or offer at least a semblance of an apology. But with rare exception, few disqualified leaders ever return to the level of effectiveness they had before being disqualified. Those few who are able to return to a prior level of effectiveness typically submit themselves to a rigorous and lengthy recovery and restoration process, including giving significant attention to accountability and the development of self-control.

The rigor of Paul's travels necessitates physical fitness. Paul faces enormous physical demands. It is estimated that he travels the equivalent of 13,400 airline miles, and if we take into account circuitous roads, that amount is significantly higher.[1] And we are reasonably certain the New Testament does not catalogue all his travels. Considering the average distance traveled in a day, the condition of ancient roads, and the rugged, sometimes mountainous terrain, we can deduce that Paul must have significant physical vitality and stamina.

In addition to a sound body, a leader needs a sound mind. Self-control is not limited to the physical realm but also includes mental focus. In addition to being physically fit, running the race well requires steady, intense concentration of focus. Runners cannot afford to become distracted by things off to the side of the course. If they do, their effectiveness in running diminishes. Staying focused requires control—not allowing distractions to interfere with the responsibility at hand. Controlling our focus goes a long way toward making the run successful.

In Romans 12, Paul comes at this issue of a sound mind from a somewhat different angle that comes into play in the individual choices we make during the course of a day. He writes, "Therefore, I urge you, brothers and sisters, in view of God's mercy, to offer your bodies as a living sacrifice, holy and pleasing to God—this is your true and proper worship. Do not conform to the pattern of this world, but be transformed by the renewing of your mind. Then you will be able to test and approve what God's will is—his good, pleasing and perfect will" (vv. 1–2). Note the link Paul makes between offering our bodies as a living sacrifice and experiencing the renewing of our mind.

Paul does not use the word "self-control" extensively in his writings, but it does appear several times in his letters to two young protégés—Timothy and Titus. Writing to Titus, Paul refers to self-control no fewer than five times (1:8; 2:2, 5, 6, 12), identifying it as a requirement for spiritual leadership in general and a prerequisite for elders to be qualified for service in the local church. He writes to Timothy about the sinful practices of the unregenerate and in the listing of sinful behavior includes the phrase "without self-control" (2 Timothy 3:3). He is reminding the young leader of the dangers that await those who lack discipline.

Leadership Lesson: It is clear that our seemingly insatiable human appetites and needs can easily lead to sinful excesses if not controlled.

The lack of self-discipline is rampant, notably in affluent societies, leading to problems like obesity, alcoholism, drug use, and debt. For leaders without self-control, our appetites for comforts and pleasures can easily become our master and lead us into sin or otherwise hinder us in our spiritual walk. If the spiritual does not govern the physical, we can become easy targets for Satan due to our lack of self-control (see 1 Corinthians 7:5).

Questions for Leadership Development

1. How is the Holy Spirit developing the fruit of self-control in your life?

2. What should you lay aside to be a better leader?

3. What aspect of your life presents the greatest challenge for self-control?

4. Should leaders be harder on themselves than they are on others, holding themselves to a higher standard?

— THIRTEEN —

HUMBLE

Do nothing out of selfish ambition or vain conceit. Rather, in humility value others above yourselves.
—Philippians 2:3

Although Paul has several notable character attributes, we are limiting our consideration to just five, including this last one—humility. Humility is often described in negative terms—*not* prideful, *not* arrogant, *not* narcissistic. To be humble is to be a person who seeks *no* reputation, *no* entitlement, *no* glory. If sin is, in essence, the corruption of the original goodness of humanity at creation, then perhaps humility *describes* the essence of the original goodness of humanity. Perhaps true humility is an indication of the absence of the corruption of sin—a person at peace with oneself, with others, and with God.

Humility is the virtue that allows an individual to have an appropriate, healthy view of self and an appropriate estimation of their own competence, accomplishments, and capabilities. As Rick Warren writes in *The Purpose-Driven Life*, humility is "not thinking less of ourselves, but thinking of ourselves *less*."[1] The humble avoid over-confidence, pride, and self-preoccupation. In an ironic twist, Moses writes about himself in the Torah, "Now Moses was a very humble man, more humble than anyone else on the face of the earth" (Numbers 12:3). How is it possible to *be* humble and also claim to be the *most* humble? Being humble is not to deny one's talents and gifts but to recognize them and use them in service to God and others. True humility, says Danielle Strickland, "is coming into agreement with what God says about you."[2]

C. S. Lewis writes in *Mere Christianity*,

Do not imagine that if you meet a really humble man he will be what most people call "humble" nowadays: he will not be a sort of greasy, smarmy person, who is always telling you that, of course, he is nobody. Probably all you will think about him is that he seemed a cheerful, intelligent chap who took a real interest in what *you* said to *him*. If you do dislike him it will be because you feel a little envious of anyone who seems to enjoy life so easily. He will not be thinking about humility: he will not be thinking about himself at all.[3]

Humility allows a leader to give the greatest consideration to the other.

Leadership Lesson: **Humble leaders talk less about themselves.**

Talking less about yourself is good for you and for the people listening to you. Carey Nieuwhof suggests, "Bragging is your insecurity leaking out."[4] Rather than highlighting their own accomplishments, humble leaders cultivate curiosity about others. Humble leaders are other-focused rather than self-focused.

No Reputation

In Philippians 2, Paul recommends an attitude of unselfish humility. He then describes how Jesus's humility is reflected in the incarnation: "But made himself of no reputation, and took upon him the form of a servant, and was made in the likeness of men" (v. 7, KJV). R. Scott Rodin suggests that true Christian leadership "is an ongoing, disciplined practice of becoming a person of no reputation, and thus, becoming more like Christ in this unique way."[5] By intent and design, Jesus leads from the posture of a servant. The prestige, prominence, power, and recognition of leadership are purposely dismissed. In his humility, Jesus makes himself *of no reputation*.

This abandonment of reputation frees a leader from the desire to be seen as significant, important, or relevant. In his reflections on Christian leadership, Henri Nouwen specifically refers to the importance of resisting the temptation to be relevant. He says, "I am deeply convinced that the Christian leader of the future is called to be completely irrelevant and to stand in this world with nothing to offer but his or her vulnerable self."[6] Such irrelevance and vulnerability demand humility and the willingness to become a leader *of no reputation*.

"No competent leader is going to be eager to impress people with their *credentials*," writes MacArthur. "Leaders who are truly able are qualified because of their *character*. They are easily identified, not by letters of commendation, but because of the influence they have on others. They are people who are confident of their calling, yet at the same time, they know they are utterly dependent on God as the source of their true power."[7]

Leadership Lesson: **Throughout history, God has chosen the least, the weak, the outcast, the untalented, the sinful, and the rejected to give great leadership at historic times.**

And usually, those leaders recognize that fact. Rodin says, "Great godly leaders have always worked at that miraculous intersection where humility and faith meet the awesome presence and power of God's Spirit."[8] At that intersection the miracle of godly leadership happens, as humble leaders of no reputation recognize their great need of God's presence and power and God supplies their need with abundant sufficiency.

No Entitlement

There is no sense of entitlement with Paul, no laying claim to something that is not rightfully his. He even disregards that which *is* his right. As an apostle, Paul may have the right to be taken care of by the church. However, he does not want to be a financial burden, so he takes a day job, using his tentmaking trade to provide for himself and his companions (see Acts 20:34–35).

When Paul and Barnabas are in Lystra, Paul heals a lame man. The miracle causes the people to think the two missionaries are gods (Acts 14:8–18). Paul and Barnabas instantly deny this misconception, shouting back at the crowd confessions of their humanity, unwilling to assume privilege and prestige they are not entitled to receive.

Leadership Lesson: **Humble leaders are not self-serving.**

A sense of entitlement is a sure sign of the absence of humility. When a leader begins to expect preferential treatment and special consideration, it becomes obvious that the leader has begun to see themselves as deserving favored status and placed themselves above others. When a leader becomes more concerned with the benefit to self over others, they have become infected with the "selfish ambition" and "vain conceit" that Paul writes about in Philippians 2:3. You'll know how much of a servant you are by how you respond when you are treated like one. Leaders are often exposed to opportunities to generate applause. But humble leaders do not seek personal gain or public praise. Their leadership reflects the ability to put others first, and they are passionate about meeting the needs of others. Their ambition is based on the common good. They use their gifts freely and appropriately, recognizing that their sufficiency is from God, not from themselves (see 2 Corinthians 3:5).

Paul is somewhat prickly about his status as an apostle; however, he is not driven by a sense of entitlement but of responsibility. He is concerned to assert the authentic character of his apostleship. While he is not eager to defend himself personally, neither is he willing to leave the Corinthian church to the wolves, so in 2 Corinthians he feels compelled to defend his own character and credentials (see references to the "super-apostles" in 11:5 and 12:11). Paul believes he is qualified as much for the status of apostle as anyone else—having personally encountered Jesus on the road to Damascus and been commissioned apostle to the gentiles. For three years, he is personally instructed in Arabia, just as the other disciples were in Judea and Galilee.

But he refuses to engage in a showy ministry of signs and wonders designed to impress. He argues that such phenomena are the opposite of true leadership, forcing the Corinthians to rethink their assumptions of what constitutes success. The desire for honor and recognition from others separates the "super-apostles" as false teachers. While Paul considers himself "less than the least of all the Lord's people" (Ephesians 3:8), he also knows that he is "not in the least inferior to those 'super-apostles'" (2 Corinthians 11:5; 12:11).

No Increase

Perhaps *the* question that determines a leader's humility is the leader's answer to the question, "Who gets the glory?" Paul gives all glory to God. He is not greedy for attention or acclaim or to increase his own popularity.

Leadership Lesson: Pride will destroy a leader's effectiveness.

Timothy Keller observes, "Pride is the carbon monoxide of sin. It silently and slowly kills you without you even knowing."[9] Pride covets ever-increasing attention and prominence. To avoid pride, leaders should stay grounded and true. Don't let success go to your head. Don't promote yourself. Don't seek the spotlight. Don't even drop hints about your own importance or your suitability for greater responsibility. Let your place of influence and leadership be determined by God.

Closely aligned to the concept of no glory is the concept of no increase. Nouwen is direct in his identification of a leader's temptation to increase: "The way of the Christian leader is not the way of upward mobility in which our world has invested so much, but the way of downward mobility ending on the cross. . . . Here we touch the most important quality of Christian leadership in the future. It is not a leadership of power and control but of powerlessness and humility in which the suffering servant of God, Jesus Christ, is made manifest."[10]

***Leadership Lesson:* Leadership bent on increasing the leader lacks integrity.**

If Christ is truly living in us, then we can in turn live for others in our work. We approach our work with deep humility and a keen awareness of our own weaknesses and shortcomings. We will have no need to seek increase of power. We will have no desire to advance our own reputation. When John the Baptist sees Jesus, he makes the declaration, "He must increase, but I must decrease" (John 3:30, NKJV). There are natural trappings that distinguish those in leadership, such as salary, title, prestige, power, influence, and honor. Each area provides tempting opportunities for increase. It is difficult to accept decrease. Shunning the perks and privileges of leadership takes great humility. Before God can do great work in an organization, that work must first be done in the heart of the leader. Humility opens the door for God to do that work.

Humility allows leaders to truly invest in and serve others for the sake *of* the other. Robert Greenleaf reminds us that the difference between a true servant–leader who is servant first, and the leader-servant who seeks leadership first, lies in the growth of the people who serve under them. The test question is, "Do those served grow as persons; do they, *while being served*, become healthier, wiser, freer, more autonomous, more likely themselves to become servants?"[11] Max De Pree's famous definition is worth repeating: "The first responsibility of the leader is to define reality. The last is to say thank you. In between, the leader is a servant."[12]

Leadership Lesson: In the end, humble leadership is all about lordship.

Before vision-casting or team-building or communication or strategic planning, humble leadership is about the lordship of Jesus Christ. Because Jesus is Lord, humble leaders sacrifice reputation, entitlement, and glory. We are called to decrease so that Jesus might increase.

Questions for Leadership Development

1. Do you want to have a great ministry, or do you just want to be great?[13] (You cannot have both.)

2. To what degree do you give God credit for your ministry success?

3. To what degree to you find yourself seeking the applause of others?

4. To what degree would those you lead say you are serving them?

5. Is it possible for humble leaders to promote themselves on social media?

PART 4

THE LEADER'S COMPETENCE

The Skill Sets that Increase a Leader's Effectiveness

Not that we are competent in ourselves to claim anything for ourselves, but our competence comes from God. He has made us competent as ministers of a new covenant—not of the letter but of the Spirit; for the letter kills, but the Spirit gives life.

—2 Corinthians 3:5–6

Trust is a function of two things: character and competence. Character includes your integrity, your motive and your intent with people. Competence includes your capabilities, your skills, and your track record. Both are vital.

—Stephen Covey, The Speed of Trust

If the character of the leader determines the leader's depth, the competencies of the leader determine the leader's breadth. In this section we will consider the various competencies of Paul's leadership—the abilities and skills that make him unusually effective as apostle to the gentiles.

The leader's competencies determine the areas in which and the degree to which leadership efforts will be successful. For example, it's difficult to imagine a pastor being effective if certain competencies are lacking, such as the ability to preach, provide pastoral care, and administrate. The same need for specific competencies is true in other professions. If Paul has a profession, it is that of apostle, and there are specific competencies critical to that vocation. Some that we will consider are universal to any leadership position—vision, strategy, communication, team-building, to name a few. But there is at least one competency that is unique to Christian leadership: being missional.

— FOURTEEN —

MISSIONAL

Now get up and stand on your feet. I have appeared to you to appoint you as a servant and as a witness of what you have seen and will see of me. I will rescue you from your own people and from the Gentiles. I am sending you to them to open their eyes and turn them from darkness to light, and from the power of Satan to God, so that they may receive forgiveness of sins and a place among those who are sanctified by faith in me.
—Acts 26:16–18

A Missional Leader

Paul is a *missional* leader. One might think that a section on Paul's leadership competencies would begin with his preaching, or teaching, or strategy. Instead, we begin with his ability to focus his attention and activity on his missionary call. The ability of a leader to be focused on the main thing is critical. For Paul's leadership, the main thing is mission.

Throughout the history of Christianity, the church has talked much about missions, missionaries, and mission fields. Now we have the word "missional," which has become a popular buzzword and spawned numerous books and articles. We can access resources on *missional* preaching, *missional* evangelism, *missional* church planting, *missional* theology, *missional* discipleship, and on it goes.

What does it mean to be a *missional* leader? It is not, as might be initially thought, simply the ability to stay on mission, though that is certainly an important aspect. To be missional is to be sent on a *specific* mission—God's mission—of redemption and reconciliation (see 2 Corinthians 5:18–20). *Missional* is a distinctly Christian term that in essence describes a missionary lifestyle. Leaders of secular organizations might be described as mission-focused or mission-driven, but they are not *missional* unless their motivation is to partner with God in the redemption of the world. Being missional includes embracing the thinking, practices, and posture of a missionary in order to reach others with the message of the gospel. To be *missional* means *mission* is the mission.

The term "missional" gained its popularity toward the end of the twentieth century with the influence of Tim Keller, Alan Hirsch, and others. Their basic premise is that all Christians should be involved in the Great Commission of Jesus, found in Matthew 28:19–20. Missional leadership refers to a leader whose single-minded focus is being an agent of God's mission to the world. In Paul's case, missional leadership means focusing on the missionary mission and developing other leaders who do the same thing. Paul's mission, simply put, is to be apostle to the gentiles.

Hirsch says that a proper understanding of missional living begins with recovering a missionary understanding of God.[1] By his very nature, God is a sending God who takes the initiative to redeem creation. This doctrine, known as *missio Dei*, has helped many redefine their understanding of the church. Because the church is composed of the sent people of God, the church is the instrument of God's mission in the world. However, most people believe that mission is an instrument of the church—a means by which the church is grown. Although Christians frequently say, "The church has a mission," a more correct statement according to missional theology would be, "The mission has a church."[2]

Missional leaders recognize that both God and the church are intrinsically and principally missionary in nature. God is a missionary (missional) God who sends a missionary (missional) church, served by missionary (missional) leaders.

A Missional Call

The first competency of leadership is knowing the mission. Is the mission to build widgets that can be sold at an affordable price? Is it to provide beds and meals for individuals experiencing homelessness? Is it to disciple a group of teenagers? In each of these cases—indeed in every case—it is possible for the mission to become hijacked by secondary concerns. This kind of misappropriation often occurs when a threat to mission achievement emerges, such as a lack of resources. Acquiring resources then subtly replaces the original mission as the leader's focus. Throughout his ministry, despite distractions and disturbances, Paul is able to remain missional because of his strong sense of call.

The story of Paul's commissioning as apostle to the gentiles is told three times in Acts (see chapters 9, 22, and 26). As we explored in chapter 3, Paul's call is a defining moment, a transforming event that determines the future trajectory of his life. When testifying during his trial, Paul succinctly summarizes the mission he has been given: "Then the Lord said to me, 'Go; I will send you far away to the Gentiles'" (Acts 22:21). When he writes to the Romans, he twice highlights the mission he has been commissioned to accomplish: "I am talking to you Gentiles. Inasmuch as I am the apostle to the Gentiles, I take pride in my ministry in the hope that I may somehow arouse my own people to envy and save some of them" (Romans 11:13–14). A few chapters later he revisits the importance of his mission: "Yet I have written you quite boldly on some points to remind you of them again, because of the grace God gave me to be a minister of Christ Jesus to the Gentiles. He gave me the priestly duty of proclaiming the gospel of God, so that the Gentiles might become an offering acceptable to God, sanctified by the Holy Spirit" (15:15–16).

Leadership Lesson: **In order to achieve the mission, leaders must know the mission.**

The missional leader is one who is aware of the mission, is focused on the mission, and is dedicated to the mission. Missional leaders have a profound sense of calling that permeates their leadership. Frederick Buechner's beautiful description of vocation—"the place God calls you to is the place where your deep gladness and the world's deep hunger meet"[3]—speaks to the importance of mission awareness.

A Missional Focus

When we speak of a leader's vision, we most often have in mind the leader's ability to comprehend the panoramic view, especially the ability to clearly see a desirable future. But an equally important component of a leader's vision is nearsightedness. The leader must be *both* farsighted *and* nearsighted—able to focus intently on the mission at hand. It may well be that the most critical aspect of a leader's vision pertains to the ability to narrowly focus on the mission despite distractions. An almost myopic, laser-like intensity is necessary to keep the mission in focus.

Leadership Lesson: **A perpetual enemy of leadership is distraction.**

Rather than being preoccupied by the challenges of criticism, conflict, and crises (or even by success and achievement), the missional leader keeps the main thing the main thing. And the main thing is the mission. One reason organizations post placards containing mission and vision statements is the need to be continually reminded to stay on track. The missional leader is focused—but focused on the right thing. It's hard to follow a distracted leader. Mission drift occurs when secondary concerns assume top priority over an extended length of time. For instance, an organization or ministry may have a cash-flow problem. Ideas for increasing cash flow are generated, and one initiative is implemented and produces the needed results. The organization or ministry then gives the successful initiative increased attention and focus, and before long the temporary initiative has become the permanent focus, and the primary mission languishes. Effective leaders avoid mission drift by keeping their focus on the principal mission.

Leaders are often tempted to take the road that is most convenient, or the option that offers the quickest return, rather than staying on mission. Paul will sacrifice methods, and he will sacrifice himself, but he will not sacrifice the mission. Even when he cannot be present in person to preach, teach, disciple, and mentor, Paul will advance the mission through letters written from prison in which he preaches, teaches, disciples, and mentors.

For Paul, being a missional leader means living as a sent one, thinking as a sent one, teaching as a sent one, and writing as a sent one for the sake of God's glory, the salvation of the lost, and the edification of the church.

Leadership Lesson: To be a missional leader requires a missional commitment.

We need apostles who draw us out to engage in mission when we'd rather hunker down and be safe. We need prophets who draw our eyes to recognize injustice when we'd rather be complacent. We need evangelists who draw us into sharing good news when we'd rather keep it to ourselves. Missional leaders help keep us all on mission for the long haul.

Questions for Leadership Development

1. What mission has God given you?

2. Have you ever drifted from your mission? If so, how did you recognize it, and what steps did you take to get back on mission?

3. What distractions keep leaders from being missional?

4. How do you determine whether your leadership is missional?

FIFTEEN

VISIONARY

*So then, King Agrippa, I was not disobedient
to the vision from heaven.*
—Acts 26:19

Vision plays a significant role in Paul's story, from the beginning
of his Christian leadership journey in Damascus, when he loses his
physical vision for a time, until his imprisonment in Rome. Paul's
physical vision, the spiritual visions he receives from the Lord, and
his leadership vision all significantly contribute to his effectiveness
as apostle to the gentiles.

Coup d'oeil is a phrase that can be useful when thinking about
vision. It is a term taken from French that refers to the ability to take
in a comprehensive view with just a glance. It is mostly used in the
military, where the *coup d'oeil* refers to the ability to discern quickly
the tactical advantages and disadvantages of the terrain. It is the gift
of being able to see at a glance all the possibilities offered by the terrain. Such ability is of great value to leaders.[1]

Leadership vision is an essential means of focusing attention on
what matters most. It begins with the skill of clearly seeing the present situation and assessing current realities. Visionary leadership involves the ability to focus intently on the mission today while also
being able to imagine the future to which God is calling both you

and those you serve. Leaders with such vision inspire us to lean into the future.

Leadership Lesson: **To be visionary, a leader needs a clear vision of both the present and the future.**

True leaders have vision—the ability to see the present as it is and imagine a future arising out of the present. Organizations often develop vision statements describing where the organization wants to go. These are helpful and have their place. However, vision statements do not necessarily translate into action and forward movement. True leadership vision is not just communicated; it is also demonstrated in the actions, beliefs, and values of the leader. Leadership vision is a mental picture in a leader's imagination that motivates people to action when it is communicated compellingly, passionately, clearly, and frequently. When vision is communicated frequently, it helps remind the leader and those they serve where they are going. It is like referencing a GPS regularly to confirm where you are and where you are headed. It is not only people who perish when there is no vision (see Proverbs 29:18, KJV). Organizations and institutions can also perish when there is an absence of vision. Long-term survival requires an inspiring image of the future that answers the question, "Where are we going?" and helps people move in that direction.

Paul's Physical Vision

Beginning with his conversion on the road to Damascus, vision is a recurring theme throughout Paul's ministry. On the road to Damascus, Paul is blinded in his life-changing encounter with Jesus. He loses his physical vision and has to be helped into the city, where he finds lodging and will spend the next three days praying.

At the same time Paul is *without* vision, Ananias experiences a vision in which he is given instructions to find Paul, lay hands on him, and restore his sight (Acts 9:10–12). When Ananias prays for Paul, what looks like scales fall from Paul's eyes and his sight is restored. Does Paul ever fully get over his Damascus blindness? We do not know for certain. In the same way that Jacob had a lingering limp (see Genesis 32:31), Paul may have also been left with a permanent reminder of his encounter with the Lord.

Paul says that he suffers from a "physical infirmity" (Galatians 4:13, NKJV) and a "thorn in my flesh" (2 Corinthians 12:7). Some biblical scholars believe that both Paul's thorn in the flesh and his physical infirmity are the same thing—his bad eyesight. Paul writes about a distressing, humiliating, physical ailment that he fears might hinder effective ministry: "Therefore, in order to keep me from becoming conceited, I was given a thorn in my flesh, a messenger of Satan, to torment me. Three times I pleaded with the Lord to take it away from me. But he said to me, 'My grace is sufficient for you, for my power is made perfect in weakness'" (2 Corinthians 12:7b–9). Three times Paul prays that the ailment be removed, and three times he is assured that grace will be supplied to bear it.

While there is no specific scripture that alludes to any other physical impairment, there are several passages that suggest poor eyesight. In Galatians 4:15, Paul makes an unusual statement: "If you could have done so, you would have torn out your eyes and given them to me." The Galatian believers so love Paul that some of them would gladly sacrifice their own eyesight in order to improve Paul's vision. Paul likely uses this statement because he has significant difficulty with his eyes.

When Paul signs the letter to the Galatians, he observes that his handwriting is recognizable because of the exceptionally large letters that he makes: "See what large letters I use as I write to you with my own hand!" (6:11). This verse, coupled with the fact that Paul nearly always uses scribes, may also suggest that he has difficulty with his sight.

In Acts 23:2–5, as Paul stands before the Jewish council in Jerusalem, he fails to recognize that he is speaking to the high priest. It is hard to imagine that Paul is not familiar with the Jewish leader; it is easier to surmise that Paul is instead unable to see him clearly.

In Acts 28:1–3 we have an account of Paul gathering firewood on Malta. When he lays a pile of brush on the fire, a snake emerges from it and bites him. Was the snake hiding in the brush pile? Was it the same color as the brush? We do not know, but we might speculate that better eyesight could've helped Paul notice it sooner.

Perhaps Paul's eyesight is strained and damaged from hours of reading and studying in poorly lighted tents. Or perhaps his stoning in Lystra has impacted his vision. Whatever the cause, we can be fairly confident that he suffers from poor eyesight.

Leadership Lesson: **A physical disability need not limit leadership potential.**

Leaders often battle physical ailments, disabilities, and sickness. While vision is critical for leadership effectiveness, sanctified imagination is of greater importance than physical eyesight. Physical disabilities provide opportunities for the sufficiency of God's grace to be manifest and for leaders to find their dependency—and their supply—in God. Far more detrimental to leadership potential than physically cloudy eyes is a spiritually cloudy heart.

Paul's Spiritual Visions

What Paul lacks in eyesight he makes up for in spiritual vision. His sight extends beyond the purely physical to the spiritual, and his physical vision is supplemented significantly by visions he has from the Lord. At least seven specific times, Paul has visions of divine origin that compensate for his physical vision and provide encouragement, assurance, and direction.

Paul's first vision occurs in Acts 9, when he encounters the risen Lord on the Damascus road, converts, and forever alters the direction of his life. He references this vision in Acts 26:19, when he testifies to King Agrippa that he has not been "disobedient to the vision from heaven."

Paul's next vision occurs three days later, while, in his blind condition, he is praying in the house of Judas (9:11–12). He has a vision of a man named Ananias coming to him and placing his hands on him to restore his sight. It brings Paul hope and assurance.

Paul's third vision occurs toward the end of Paul's time in Tarsus. Before he goes to Antioch, he has a strange experience that leaves its mark on him for the rest of his life. He gives an account of it in 2 Corinthians 12:1–4:

> I must go on boasting. Although there is nothing to be gained, I will go on to visions and revelations from the Lord. I know a man in Christ who fourteen years ago was caught up to the third heaven. Whether it was in the body or out of the body I do not know—God knows. And I know that this man—whether in the body or apart from the body I do not know, but God knows—was caught up to paradise and heard inexpressible things, things that no one is permitted to tell.

Paul describes this incredible vision in vague terms. It is a mystical, ecstatic experience difficult to put into words, and Paul freely admits he doesn't understand it. In his account he stands outside the experience and relates it as if it happened to a third party. Though fourteen years have passed since the vision, the experience is still vividly remembered, as though the vision so fills Paul with transforming glory that the glow still remains years later.

Paul's fourth vision is recounted in Acts 16:9–10 and is commonly called the Macedonian vision. While at Troas, Paul has a vision of a Macedonian man "standing and begging him, 'Come over to Macedonia and help us'" (v. 9). It is a vision that provides Paul with direction and a sense of urgency, and as a result the gospel spreads to Europe.

Paul's fifth vision occurs while he is in Corinth, recounted in Acts 18:9–10: "One night the Lord spoke to Paul in a vision: 'Do not be afraid; keep on speaking, do not be silent. For I am with you, and no one is going to attack and harm you, because I have many people in this city.'" This vision gives Paul the confidence to continue to proclaim the gospel.

Paul's sixth vision occurs when he falls into a trance at the temple in Jerusalem. Paul is instructed, "Leave Jerusalem immediately, because the people here will not accept your testimony about me" (22:18). God uses this vision to provide Paul with clear direction and a sense of urgency.

Paul's final vision occurs in the midst of a terrible storm while he and his companions sail toward Rome. In this vision, an angel assures Paul with these words: "Do not be afraid, Paul. You must stand trial before Caesar; and God has graciously given you the lives of all who sail with you" (27:24). The vision provides needed encouragement and assurance, and it is proven true, despite the subsequent shipwreck.

Leadership Lesson: Visions from God are gifts given at God's discretion.

There are times when God imparts special revelation to God's leaders. At times of God's own choosing, he stimulates the leader's imagination to see a desirable future. This sense of vision for the future seems to come to leaders most often in the context of prayer, Bible study, or times of personal reflection. While Paul's physical vision may be fuzzy and suspect, his spiritual visions bring great clarity and direction to his life.

Paul's Leadership Vision

The apostle Paul is possessed by a missional vision that drives him to be the greatest missionary of the early church and of Christian history. Paul's leadership vision is not literal vision but metaphorical. He *sees* the spread of the gospel before it becomes reality then travels thousands of miles to fulfill his calling to "be a minister of Christ Jesus to the Gentiles" (Romans 15:16). This vision underlies his ambition to take the good news as far away as Spain (see Romans 15:20, 23–24).

Paul has the ability to clearly see both what is and what needs to be. He has the capacity to imagine what does not yet exist—gentile communities of Christian faith—and to recognize possibilities for seeing the vision become reality.

Leadership Lesson: Leadership vision is the ability to see both what does exist and also what does not yet exist.

Perhaps visionary leadership can best be described, in the words of A. W. Tozer, as "sanctified imagination."[2] Vision is absolutely crucial to leadership. Warren Bennis, an American pioneer in leadership studies, defines leadership as "the capacity to create a compelling vision and translate it into action and sustain it." He goes on to say that, "with a vision, the leader provides the all-important bridge from the present to the future of the organization."[3]

Questions for Leadership Development

1. What is the vision statement of your organization or ministry?

2. What is your vision or mission statement for your own life and family?

3. Is it easier for you to assess the present or imagine the future?

4. Describe a vision you have received from the Lord.

5. What is the relationship between leadership vision and sanctified imagination?

— SIXTEEN —

STRATEGIC

As was his custom, Paul went into the synagogue, and on three Sabbath days he reasoned with them from the Scriptures.
—Acts 17:2

As we explored in the previous chapter, vision is incredibly important to effective leadership. But vision is not enough. A detailed strategy is needed to implement vision. The ability to develop and implement strategy is a competency necessary for vision to become reality. Strategy is the route we take to arrive at the destination described by the vision.

To fulfill his vision, Paul employs appropriate and effective strategies. The general strategy includes starting churches, strengthening churches, and developing leaders. In this chapter, we will focus on Paul's primary strategy of *starting* churches.[1]

Leadership Lesson: If vision is the destination, then strategy is the various components that get you there.

Some of the components of reaching a destination include the route, the means, intermediate destinations, addressing various challenges along the road, the people who will travel with you, and how you will be sustained on the journey.

The Journeys

For Paul, the initial component of his church-planting strategy is the determination to be itinerant—to *travel* to spread the gospel. As an apostle, Paul says his work is "to preach the gospel where it had not been heard before and to plant churches where none had existed before."[2] As an itinerant missionary, Paul embarks on distinct journeys. He travels along Roman highways—the main lines of transit and communication—preaching the gospel and planting churches in strategic centers. From those centers, the gospel message spreads.

The first missionary journey will differ from the second and third journeys in that the length of travel will be about half. The first journey will begin and end with travel by sea, while the next two journeys will begin with travel by land and end with travel by sea. The latter approach will provide for a time of rest aboard ship as Paul makes his way back to Antioch, and the sailing will be easier with the prevailing westerly winds.

First Missionary Journey

Paul's first missionary journey is recorded in Acts 13 and 14. In approximately AD 47, while the church in Antioch (in Syria) is fasting and worshiping, the Holy Spirit says, "Set apart for me Barnabas and [Paul] for the work to which I have called them" (13:2). So, after praying and laying their hands on them, the church in Antioch sends Paul and Barnabas on their first missionary journey.

The missionary team first sails to the island of Cyprus, which is Barnabas's home territory. They arrive at Salamis and teach in several synagogues along with John Mark. They then set sail from Paphos to go to Perga (in modern-day Turkey) while John Mark sets sail to return to Jerusalem.

From Perga, Paul and Barnabas make their way to Antioch in Pisidia (rather than the Antioch in Syria), where they teach in the synagogue, and many believe. Eventually driven out of Antioch by the Jews, Paul and Barnabas make their way to Iconium and teach in the synagogue there. Many believe, but over time, the city becomes divided between those who follow the Jews and those who side with the apostles. When Paul and Barnabas learn that their opposition is planning to stone them, they flee to Lystra, Derbe, and the surrounding area.

In Lystra, Paul performs a miracle that results in people believing that he and Barnabas are gods. They immediately correct the misperception. Then Jews from Antioch in Pisidia and Iconium arrive and persuade the crowds to stone Paul, after which he is dragged out of the city and left for dead. However, when the disciples gather around him, he gets up and limps back into Lystra. The next day, he and Barnabas travel to Derbe and share the gospel. Many more become disciples.

Upon completing their time teaching in Derbe, Paul and Barnabas retrace their steps, returning through Lystra, to Iconium, and to Antioch in Pisidia to encourage the believers and appoint elders in each church before making the trip home to Antioch in Syria. On the way to Antioch, they pass through Perga and set sail from Attalia, taking the time to share the gospel in both places.

The entire missionary journey is believed to have taken twelve to eighteen months. In Antioch, Paul and Barnabas report to the church "all that God had done through them and how he had opened a door of faith to the Gentiles" (14:27).

Leadership Lesson: We learn several things from Paul's first missionary journey.

We learn how God calls and the church confirms individuals to become missionaries, the importance of having ministry partners, the need to set realistic expectations that not everyone will accept the gospel message, the need to develop leaders in groups of new believers, the importance of checking in on them periodically, and the importance of reporting back to those who have prayed for you. This first missionary journey not only results in the spread of the gospel and the planting of churches, but it also helps prepare Paul for the journeys that will follow.

Second Missionary Journey

Paul's second missionary journey is recorded in Acts 15:36–18:22. A year or two after completing their first journey, Paul suggests that he and Barnabas revisit the churches they planted. A sharp disagreement arises over whether John Mark, who left them on the first journey, should join them on this one. Eventually Barnabas decides to take John Mark to Cyprus while Paul takes Silas to modern-day Turkey.

Paul and Silas make their way through Syria, Cilicia, and Derbe, strengthening the churches. They pick up Timothy, a young but highly regarded believer, in Lystra. The three men continue to travel, town to town through Galatia, and the number of new believers increases daily. They desire to enter Asia to spread the gospel there, but the Holy Spirit prevents them. Finally, in Troas, Paul receives a vision of a man asking them to go into Macedonia (modern-day Greece).

Paul, Silas, and Timothy are joined by Luke, and they sail from Troas to Greece, reaching the European mainland, and make their way to Philippi. In Philippi, the wealthy merchant Lydia opens her heart to the gospel and her home as a meeting place. Later, Paul and Silas are beaten and thrown in prison, but a providential earthquake brings about their release. The next morning, the magistrates free Paul and Silas, and they rejoin Timothy to travel to Thessalonica.

Paul preaches in the synagogue in Thessalonica, and some Jews believe as well as many Greeks, including some of the leading women. Unfortunately, the non-believing Jews form a violent mob, and Paul and Silas escape by night to Berea. Timothy spends time in Thessalonica to establish and exhort the new believers in their faith, and he later brings Paul an encouraging report on the status of their walk with God (1 Thessalonians 3:2–6).

In Berea, Paul again shares the gospel in the synagogue, and many believe. Unfortunately, the non-believing Jews from Thessalonica arrive in Berea to stir up trouble, and Paul sails off to Athens by himself while Timothy and Silas stay behind.

When Paul reaches Athens, he preaches both in the synagogue and in the marketplace and is eventually invited to give a speech to the Areopagus. Some Athenians believe, others mock, and still more seem interested only in intellectual stimulation, so Paul continues on to Corinth.

In Corinth, Paul meets fellow Jews and tentmakers Priscilla and Aquila and decides to stay and work with them. He begins his year-and-a-half-long ministry in Corinth by teaching in the synagogue and is soon joined by Silas and Timothy. During his time in Corinth, Paul writes 1 and 2 Thessalonians.

When it is time to return to Antioch in Syria, Priscilla and Aquila accompany Paul as he sails to Ephesus and shares the gospel there. Priscilla and Aquila settle in Ephesus while Paul sails on to Caesarea. He then makes his way to his home church in Antioch and shares what God has done in the course of his travels.

Leadership Lesson: There are things we can learn from Paul's second missionary journey.

We see that God can bring good results even out of a "sharp disagreement" like the one Barnabas and Paul have when they split up and go in different directions, sharing the gospel in new places (see Acts 15:39–40). Paul and Silas show that it's possible to praise God even in hard times when they continue to praise God from their jail cell in Philippi after a serious beating. And we see God's providence in providing partners in ministry like Priscilla and Aquila.

Third Missionary Journey

After updating his home church in Antioch in Syria about the things God did during his second journey, Paul departs again on a third journey to strengthen the churches he has previously planted. This journey is recorded in Acts 18:23–21:17.

Paul travels through Galatia, visiting the churches in Derbe, Lystra, Iconium, and Antioch in Pisidia, which he planted during his first missionary journey. He then goes to Ephesus, where he spends three months preaching in the synagogue, then the next two years in fruitful ministry to the gentiles in the city.

Led by the Holy Spirit to continue his missionary journey, Paul sends Timothy and Erastus ahead to Macedonia. After a riot takes place in Ephesus, Paul bids farewell to the disciples there and sails to Macedonia, where he writes his second letter to the Corinthians while visiting the churches in Philippi, Thessalonica, and Berea before finally making his way to Corinth.

After three months in Corinth, where Paul writes the letter to the Romans, he plans to sail to Syria. However, he discovers a plot by the non-believing Jews to waylay him on the voyage, so he decides instead to return through Macedonia, retracing his steps through Berea, Thessalonica, and Philippi. In Philippi, he meets up with Luke. The two then set sail for Troas, where they meet up with traveling companions on their way to Jerusalem from various churches. These church representatives are bringing monetary gifts to the persecuted church in Jerusalem. They spend one week in Troas, and on the final day Paul preaches late into the night. A young man, Eutychus, who has been listening from a third-story windowsill, falls asleep and plunges to the ground below, where he dies. Paul raises Eutychus from the dead, serves Communion, and continues preaching until daybreak.

Paul walks to Assos while the rest of the traveling companions sail to that port and take Paul aboard. They sail to Miletus near Ephesus, making a few stops along the way. Paul is in a hurry to arrive in Jerusalem in time for Pentecost, so rather than visit Ephesus, where he might feel compelled to stay longer than he wishes, he asks the elders of the church in Ephesus to meet him in Miletus for a final word of encouragement and farewell.

Paul, Luke, and their companions then continue to sail to Tyre in Syria, making short stops in Kos, Rhodes, and Patara along the way. They stay in Tyre seven days. Many disciples there urge Paul not to go into Jerusalem, where he is sure to face persecution. Paul, however, continues on his journey, sailing to Ptolemais then to Caesarea. During his stay in Caesarea, a Jewish prophet named Agabus prophesies that Paul will be bound and delivered into the hands of the gentiles when he reaches Jerusalem. Paul is not dissuaded by the prophecy, and he enters Jerusalem, where the fellow believers receive him and his companions gladly. Thus ends Paul's third missionary journey around AD 56, approximately four years after he left his home church in Antioch in Syria.

Leadership Lesson: Paul's third missionary journey provides several examples for leaders.

His emphasis on visiting churches he planted shows the importance of reconnecting with and encouraging new believers. Paul's reliance on the Holy Spirit to direct his travel plans and tell him when to move on exemplifies the extent to which all leaders should trust God's direction. Paul's time in Tyre, where he refuses to be discouraged from following God's plan, is an example to stand firm against opposition. In systematic ways and through unexpected opportunities, the gospel spreads.

Fourth and Fifth Journeys

Paul's "fourth missionary journey"[3] begins after he is arrested in Jerusalem and pleads his case before three tribunals. Having appealed to Caesar, he will cross the Mediterranean, saving the passengers and crew who become shipwrecked and winning the affection of the entire island of Malta before finally reaching Rome.

There is potentially a fifth journey that Paul takes—to Spain—before being taken back to Rome for martyrdom.

The Cities

The destinations along Paul's journeys are intentional and strategic. Although Paul visits a significant number of cities in his travels, there are a few in which he spends extended time establishing churches and developing leaders. He identifies key, vital centers from which the gospel can filter out to other towns and villages. He settles in these key cities for extensive work in hopes of reaching the region. For instance, he chooses Philippi to reach out to Macedonia, Corinth for Achaia, and Ephesus for Asia Minor. These gentile population centers are major crossroads, and Paul spends extra time in each of them, relying on the movement of people and trade in and out of the cities to help spread the gospel.

Philippi

Paul first visits Philippi on his second journey (see Acts 16:11–12) and baptizes the first few believers there. Philippi has no synagogue, which means fewer than ten male Jews live there. But even in Philippi, Paul starts with a gathering of Jews. Since the city is absent the usual launching pad for Paul's ministry, he and his companions seek out the open-air gathering of Jews on the Sabbath, outside the city walls near the river. Lydia, from Thyatira, responds to Paul's message. She and her household are baptized, and her home becomes the base of ministry in the city.

On this first visit Paul ends up in a Philippian jail with Silas. When Paul casts demons out of an enslaved girl, her owners—who profited monetarily from her condition—start a riot, and Paul and Silas are brought before the city magistrates for what they have done. They are severely beaten and thrown in prison,[4] but they continue to praise God from their jail cell. That night, God causes an earthquake to release all the prisoners, but none flee. Because the prisoners stay, Paul is able to share the gospel with the jailer, who believes and is baptized. In the morning, the magistrates free Paul and Silas, but Paul refuses to leave without a public apology for the way his rights as a Roman citizen have been violated. The magistrates hurry to the prison and offer humble apologies. Since it is earlier than Paul planned to leave, and the believers are not sufficiently mature, he leaves Luke to continue to disciple them. Paul, Silas, and Timothy then travel to Thessalonica (see 16:11–17:1).

Paul is in Philippi again about five years later while on his third journey, and once more on his return journey (see 20:1–2, 6).

Paul's letter to the Philippians is probably written about AD 61, while Paul is under house arrest in Rome. At that point he has known some of the people he is writing to for more than ten years. From that letter, it seems Paul also intends to visit Philippi again after he is released (see Philippians 2:24).

Corinth

Corinth is one of the most fruitful mission fields Paul visits. Located southwest of Athens, Corinth is the capital of Achaia and one of the largest cities Paul encounters. The urban concentration, marked by sexual appetites and superstition, is described by John Pollock as "the most populated, wealthy, commercial-minded, and sex-obsessed city in western Europe."[5]

A large, cosmopolitan city, Corinth has commercial advantages, prosperity, and a reputation for luxury, sexual laxity, and immorality. Ritual fornication has become so deeply ingrained that "to Corinthianize" is a synonym for being sexually immoral. "A Corinthian girl" is a euphemism for prostitute.

Corinth holds a strategic position, commanding two waterways, which provides the city a trade advantage as many wares pass through. Paul, ever the strategist, seizes upon this opportunity to establish a church not only in a city with a teeming population but also in a city from which the seeds of the gospel can easily spread both east and west.

At first, Paul is hindered by the absence of his team and his need to earn a living. He meets fellow Jews and tentmakers Aquila and Priscilla and decides to stay and work with them. He begins his year-and-a-half-long ministry in Corinth by teaching in the synagogue. When Silas and Timothy arrive, things pick up steam quickly. One would think Paul's work in the Corinthian synagogue would cause riots, as it has in other places, but Crispus, the ruler of the synagogue, becomes a believer, which helps Paul's cause and provides hope.

When the Corinthian Jews do begin to oppose Paul, he turns his attention to the gentiles and transitions to a house across the street provided by a gentile named Justus. Many Corinthian gentiles believe and are baptized. During his time in Corinth, Paul writes 1 and 2 Thessalonians. He also receives a vision from God encouraging him to continue preaching the gospel despite upcoming hardship. After this vision, the Jews bring Paul before the proconsul Gallio, arguing that Paul is teaching worship contrary to the Law. Gallio refuses to hear the case without Paul having to speak a word in his own defense. The result is that Sosthenes, the new ruler of the synagogue, is seized by the Greeks and beaten, and Paul continues in Corinth a little longer (see Acts 18). Amazingly, sometime after this episode, Sosthenes becomes a follower of Jesus and a fellow worker with Paul (see 1 Corinthians 1:1).

Paul labors for a year and a half with marvelous results. If Philippi is his most joyful place of service, Corinth is his most fruitful—and what a variety of fruit! While there are some influential converts (Crispus, Gaius, Stephanus), most of them "were of the lowest caste, and of those who had been deeply stained with the vices that made Corinth notorious."[6] Corinth proves that Christianity can take root in an urban center (metropolis) then spread throughout the province.[7]

Ephesus

Ephesus is the third-largest city in the Roman Empire. The Ephesian temple of the Greek goddess Artemis stands as one of the seven wonders of the ancient world. If Corinth is sex-obsessed, then Ephesus is enthralled by the magic arts and the occult.

Paul's first visit to Ephesus, toward the end of his second missionary journey, is brief. He visits the synagogue once, declining their invitation to stay, and promises to return "if it is God's will" (Acts 18:21). He leaves Priscilla and Aquila in Ephesus to establish the work and sails to Caesarea, on his way Jerusalem.

Early in his third missionary journey, Paul returns to Ephesus to fulfill his promise and stays between two and three years. As he begins ministry in Ephesus, he disciples twelve men who, possibly previously taught by Apollos, are aware only of John's baptism. Since the twelve men have received limited Christian teaching, Paul supplies what has been lacking. The men are baptized "in the name of the Lord Jesus" and receive the Holy Spirit (19:5–6).

Paul spends three months preaching in the synagogue in Ephesus, but when resistance builds, Paul withdraws with the disciples and begins having "discussions daily in the lecture hall of Tyrannus" (v. 9). He continues teaching and doing extraordinary miracles there for two years until all the people in the area have heard the word of the Lord. Paul also writes 1 Corinthians during this time in Ephesus.

The city is renowned throughout the world for the worship of Diana and the practice of magic, and Paul's ministry has a negative impact on both. The popularity of this new religion concerns some people in Ephesus, specifically the silversmith Demetrius and others who make a living crafting and selling statues of the goddess Artemis. They find their way of life threatened by Paul's preaching. A mob gathers, and Demetrius incites a riot. After several hours, the town clerk is able to quiet the crowd and send everyone home, instructing them to bring their grievances against Paul to court for a proper hearing. Soon after, Paul sets out for Macedonia, likely leaving Timothy in Ephesus to provide leadership to the growing community of believers.

Paul's last meeting with the elders of Ephesus takes place at Miletus while Paul is hurrying to Jerusalem at the end of his third missionary journey. From his tearful farewell address to his Ephesian friends, we learn that his voice had not been heard within the school of Tyrannus alone but that he had gone about among his converts, instructing them from house to house (see Acts 20:17–38).

While under house arrest in Rome, Paul will send three letters to the city of Ephesus: 1 Timothy, 2 Timothy, and Ephesians.

Leadership Lesson: Paul's strategy involves focus and multiplication.

Paul focuses on and settles in a center to reach a region,[8] then reaches it through converts who multiply converts. Through this strategy, Paul makes disciples who make disciples.

The Synagogues

When Paul visits a city, his preferred place to start is the synagogue, where he uses Scripture and his own personal experience of Jesus to explain and prove the gospel. He typically meets with a mixed response. Some are receptive; others show anger and hostility. The latter response usually wins out, as jealousy among the Jewish leaders rises to the point where Paul and his companions are either beaten, imprisoned, forced to escape in the darkness of night, or all of the above. It is said that, upon entering a city, Paul asks where the synagogue is and where the jail is because he usually starts in one and ends up in the other. Occasionally, Paul finds a sympathetic audience in a synagogue, as in Pisidian Antioch. But even there, the good favor does not last long.

Synagogues are established in most of the large cities of the empire as a result of the Jewish dispersion. They contribute to the continuity of the Jewish people by maintaining a unique identity and way of worship. They are gathering places for Jews who live in cities, places where Torah is taught. The synagogues provide a natural affiliation for Paul and suggest that Paul can begin with the Old Testament in his proclamation of Jesus.

Invariably, the Jews reject the gospel while the gentiles welcome it. Paul interprets this occurrence as the original olive branches being broken off, while wild branches are grafted in. The typical routine is that Paul arrives in a city, preaches in the synagogue, receives

Jewish opposition, produces fruit in gentile ministry, faces Jewish threats and disturbances, and experiences expulsion by mob violence or judicial process just when the gospel gains a hold.

Starting in the synagogues is a matter of principle, not prudence. It causes Paul more pain and sorrow than not doing so, but he owes his fellow Jews the opportunity to hear about Jesus and believe. In theory, the Jews are the most likely audience to respond favorably to the gospel message, and the synagogues give him a connection for potential believers. In reality, many more gentiles than Jews convert under Paul's ministry. But Paul takes it for granted that the gospel is to be presented "first to the Jew" (Romans 1:16).

Questions for Leadership Development

1. Which comes easier for you, vision or strategy?

2. What strategies are you presently employing to achieve mission and vision?

3. What components of Paul's strategy do you find most intriguing?

— SEVENTEEN —

TEAM-BUILDING

Therefore encourage one another and build each other up,
just as in fact you are doing.
—1 Thessalonians 5:11

Peter and John dominate the first twelve chapters of Acts. Then the focus swings to Paul and Barnabas in chapter 13. Over the next several chapters, Paul is joined by Mark, Silas, Timothy, Aquila, Priscilla, Luke, and Aristarchus as he builds a team of gifted and graced leaders. In addition to these, there are fellow ministers in every church Paul establishes. Paul's leadership is never depicted as a one-person show. John MacArthur notes, "The undeniable biblical pattern is for multiple elders, team leadership, and shared responsibility."[1] A key competency of Paul's leadership is his ability to identify, recruit, organize, develop, and deploy an effective team.

Teamwork is the deliberate collaboration between people endeavoring together to achieve the same goal. Team-building is the assembling and utilization of a variety of individuals who will work together to achieve collectively what cannot be achieved individually. Paul's efforts are almost always collective ventures involving a team of key coworkers across the areas he travels.

Leadership Lesson: Leadership is essentially the process of team-building.

Experienced leaders must be competent in identifying and inviting emerging leaders to be part of the team, and then developing, empowering, and deploying those leaders. Effective teams are built as experienced leaders invest in emerging leaders. This results in the greater success of the churches, ministries, and organizations being served, and the increased accomplishment of the mission. The more we cultivate people to help achieve the mission and the more we learn to delegate, the better we lead. Great teamwork provides a visible illustration of people who are united with the same purpose. Ultimately, your church, ministry, or organization should be seeking to build a culture of many people united in the mission.

Identifying and Recruiting Leaders

Building a team is a key component of strategic leadership and an early strategic step toward achieving the mission. People are the most valuable resource a leader can cultivate. Richard Ascough and Charles Cotton suggest that, for Paul, "Winning individual souls is not the sole focus; building a winning community is."[2] The first step in building community is building the team that models community.

Paul often relies on indigenous (locally raised) leadership for the organization of his churches, a practice that is reflective of the missionary principle that *the best seed comes from the harvest.* His strategy is, first, to preach the gospel to win converts and, second, to disciple the converts to become leaders who disciple other converts. As Paul spends time discipling the new converts, he is able to discern their gifts and abilities and recognize where they might best fit on the team.

Paul is a team builder, continually recruiting individuals to be part of the team. He is always on the lookout for potential and emerging leaders. His relationship-based strategy crosses social, cultural, and geographic boundaries. An example of this is the diversity of the team that delivers the offering for the needy saints in Jerusalem. Accompanying Paul with the collection are Timothy of Lystra, Sopater of Berea, and Gaius of Derbe, representing Galatia. Aristarchus and Secundus are Thessalonians. Trophimus and Tychicus, both Greeks, are from Asia (see Acts 20:4).

Paul operates with a pattern of multiple elders, shared responsibility, and team leadership. The ability to build community is a relational process in which everyone in the community is engaged. Virtually every time elders are spoken of in Scripture in connection with a church, the noun is plural, clearly indicating that the standard practice in the New Testament is for multiple elders to oversee each church. There is a plurality of leadership—every ministry is described as a team effort.

Leadership Lesson: The more diverse the team, the greater the potential.

Several years ago, I had the privilege of observing a team of incredibly diverse leaders in a meeting in which they were individually reporting, then collectively shaping strategies for continued mission success. The team had responsibility for a diverse region of the world, and the make-up of the team reflected the diversity of the region, reflecting many cultures and multiple leadership styles. Some had hard edges and forceful, direct personalities. Those leaders were serving in places where the ground was hard and a heavy plow was needed to successfully break up the soil in order to create even the possibility of producing fruit. Others were tactful and nuanced, serving in areas that were cosmopolitan, cultured, and refined—requiring leaders with diplomacy who could lead primarily through influence rather than force of personality. The leader who recruited and developed the team was himself highly competent, able to bring order to the chaos of multi-layered team dynamics. The best teams are collections of people with diverse skills, combining the varied talents and backgrounds of diverse individuals and appreciating the gifts that each one contributes. Great teams have people who both know their own role and appreciate the roles of others.

Assigning Responsibility

Paul has the competence to discern who is gifted and graced to become the overseer of Ephesus and who has the ability and responsibility needed to deliver and explain the epistle to the Romans. He is able to determine what responsibilities are best suited to which leaders and whose gifts fit where. Some of Paul's converts become leaders who continue to serve where they are discovered. Others are sent to distant places. We don't know what process Paul employs for determining who will do what, but it is obvious that he is gifted in this regard and that his method of assigning responsibility is effective.

Real teamwork always involves a bit of chaos and the clash of ideas. The context of Paul's work—including both the constraints of Roman rule and the conflicts with Jewish authorities—makes for a significant challenge in organizing a team that will be effective in the mission. Add to that the significant diversity of Paul's team—both gentiles and Jews from different continents—and the building of community will require significant competence.

Leadership Lesson: Leaders have to learn to adapt to a bit of chaos if the team is to be effective.

Richard Ascough and Charles Cotton introduce the concept of Paul as a "chaordic" leader.[3] The classic model of organizational management is a well-oiled machine that results in the smooth operation of an organization. Ascough and Cotton suggest that a different model is needed that understands that most organizations evolve with complex systems and complex relationships that result in chaos. The term "chaos" does not refer to confusion, disarray, or pandemonium but to "a complex, unpredictable, and orderly disorder in which patterns of behavior unfold in irregular but similar forms."[4] Dee Hock, founder of the VISA credit card company, first coined the term "chaordic." Hock illustrates how hierarchical command-and-control institutions alienate and dishearten people within them. He writes, "The organization of the future will be the embodiment of community based on shared purpose calling to the higher aspirations of people."[5] Hock goes on to define a new vision of institutional organization. A chaordic organization harmoniously combines characteristics of both chaos and order, immensely complex and chaotic, but also requiring cohesion and coherence, or order.

Paul is able to be a chaordic leader—providing organizational structure that reflects both order and chaos. His organization is strategic enough to achieve the kind of success that is possible only by sticking to a dynamic plan, and nimble enough to respond to spontaneous opportunities and crises as they arise.

Shaping and Nurturing Leaders

New organizations, churches, and ministries typically have fragile beginnings, especially if begun in a context of cultural turbulence, as are Paul's church plants. They must be carefully nurtured through stages of development. Paul must know when to apply pressure and how much in order to best shape young leaders and fledgling churches.

In some ways, Paul is an abrasive leader. He has the reputation of sometimes being prickly and confrontational. But he also has the capacity to be vulnerable and tender. His leadership brings both capabilities to bear as needed, and he shows graceful finesse or hardy grit as situations merit.

Leadership Lesson: Teams are often shaped through abrasive encounters.

Ascough and Cotton suggest the metaphor of sandpaper to describe the ways abrasive encounters can shape teams and leaders.[6] Sandpaper does its job by being abrasive. The grit, the amount of pressure applied, and whether it is used on green wood or seasoned wood become important factors in determining whether the process will bring out the wood's natural beauty or mar its surface. The essential skill is knowing how much roughness and pressure to use. Sandpaper can teach us how to deal with people too. The pressure and grit that can bring out the beauty in some people can irreversibly scar others. The leader who holds the sandpaper must be wise and discerning in how it is applied.

Paul is already in relationship with the Galatians when he writes the letter that bears their name. He can be more abrasive with them because the relationship is well established—in this case, the wood is seasoned. Paul also uses firm pressure and coarse sandpaper when dealing with Peter: "But when Peter was come to Antioch, I withstood him to the face, because he was to be blamed" (Galatians 2:11, KJV). In this instance, Paul is going against the grain, and a heavier hand is needed.

Paul uses a light touch and fine sandpaper when dealing with Euodia and Syntyche: "I plead with Euodia and I plead with Syntyche to be of the same mind in the Lord" (Philippians 4:2). A brief mention—a light touch—is all that is needed in this case to encourage reconciliation.[7]

Paul refers to his previous letter to the Corinthians in 2 Corinthians 7:8–9. He says he is not sorry for the hard things he wrote in the previous letter because it led them to repentance. In the earlier letter, Paul showed tough love. But 2 Corinthians provides a lighter touch in which Paul shows tender love.

In Acts 14:22, Paul is "strengthening the disciples and encouraging them to remain true to the faith." The Thessalonians also experience his tenderness when he writes, "For you know that we dealt with each of you as a father deals with his own children, encouraging, comforting and urging you to live lives worthy of God, who calls you into his kingdom and glory" (1 Thessalonians 2:11–12). Paul knows the value of offering encouragement.

Paul knows when to nudge and when to push, when to use a heavy hand and when a light touch will do. He knows the value of an encouraging word to nurture the team. Leaders are often surprised to discover how well people respond to an encouraging word. Like water refreshes a wilted flower, an encouraging word can have an invigorating effect on people.

Leadership Lesson: The development and shaping of leaders is a never-ending process.

People don't mysteriously and suddenly reach their potential without being nurtured. True leaders develop people toward reaching their full potential with encouraging words, helpful counsel, and supportive interactions. Great organizations, great ministries, and great businesses develop cultures that build people up.

Paul's strategic approach to mission is also illustrated in the way he mentors and trains individuals with leadership potential. He is no lone ranger but instead always takes others with him on his missionary journeys. Furthermore, he doesn't engage in drive-by evangelism but establishes churches where his converts can be discipled and grow in their faith. Before he leaves a church, he ensures that there are appropriate leadership structures in place. He also continues to nurture and encourage these new churches through return visits and letters.

Leadership Lesson: **Leaders develop other leaders.**

The mission does not succeed unless leaders are being developed. Two great tools for shaping and nurturing emerging leaders are modeling and mentoring. Paul models leadership for the young leaders accompanying him on his journeys. As they observe the ways Paul interacts with those to whom he presents the gospel, his discipling of new converts, and his response to significant challenges, they are being prepared for such leadership themselves. Followers will only grow as strong and deep as the leader. Paul's mentoring of emerging leaders like Timothy and Titus inspires them to reach their full potential. He builds confidence in others by observing their ministry and speaking truth and grace into their lives.

Releasing Leaders

Beginning with his first missionary journey, Paul is preparing and positioning leaders for significant responsibility. Everywhere they travel, "Paul and Barnabas appointed elders for them in each church" (Acts 14:23). They delegate leadership to trusted people. And at the conclusion of his missionary journeys, Paul is still developing and deploying leaders. He writes to Titus, "The reason I left you in Crete was that you might put in order what was left unfinished and appoint elders in every town, as I directed you" (Titus 1:5).

Leadership Lesson: **Team-building leaders need a loose grip.**

Having a loose grip on responsibility allows leaders to delegate. Delegation is an indispensable component of developing leaders and building a team.[8] Good leaders prepare their replacements by providing training, guidance, oversight, and feedback, then delegate significant responsibilities to them. This is how leaders nurture the growth of a team.

A team-building leader is competent in delegation. Having a loose grip on individuals allows experienced leaders to deploy emerging leaders. The willingness to allow young leaders to develop their own teams, rather than limiting them to your team, provides opportunities for both the young leader and the organization to grow.

Paul has a large, effective team. These are the people to whom he delegates responsibility, in whom he places his trust, and on whom he depends. Paul shows great competence in the way he identifies, recruits, organizes, develops, and deploys an effective team.

Questions for Leadership Development

1. What teams have you been on that most contributed to your development as a leader?

2. What is the process for identifying, recruiting, and developing leaders in your organization?

3. If your leader were to ask you how you are best encouraged, how would you respond?

4. Do you thrive in conditions that reflect chaos or in conditions that reflect order?

5. Does your leadership style most reflect a loose grip or a clenched fist?

EIGHTEEN

DECISIVE

Since we live by the Spirit, let us keep in step with the Spirit.
—Galatians 5:25

Decisiveness—a leader's ability to make decisions in a timely manner—is an indispensable competency of effective leadership. Decisive leaders display an ability to act, to choose a direction and a pace, and to execute strategies and plans in an appropriate timeframe. Decisiveness is a competency that Paul displays over and over again as he determines where to go next, how long to stay, and when and to whom to delegate responsibility.

Leadership Lesson: **A crucial aspect of being an effective leader is the ability to make decisions that are time sensitive and well informed.**

Decisive leaders have the ability to balance the risk of delaying a decision while continuing to gather information versus the cost of making a choice too quickly that proves to be a poor decision. Such balancing can result in paralysis if the leader defers making a timely decision. An indecisive leader can be frustrating to the rest of the team since indecision can slow momentum, lose out on timely opportunities, and cause mission initiatives to languish. Decisiveness is key to effectively executing plans, achieving set goals, and keeping the team engaged.

Spirit-led Discernment

If decision-making is to be effective, discernment is a necessary ingredient—the ability to clearly see the aspects to be considered and recognize the probable consequences of actions being considered. Discernment is gained through prayer, thoughtful reflection, and by learning to recognize the leading of the Holy Spirit. Through prayer, leaders can become attuned to the leading of the Spirit.

Paul's prayers that the churches to whom he writes would have wisdom and revelation are indicative that he is probably praying the same for himself. He prays for the Ephesians that God "may give you the Spirit of wisdom and revelation, so that you may know him better. I pray that the eyes of your heart may be enlightened" (Ephesians 1:17b–18a). Paul writes the Colossians, "We continually ask God to fill you with the knowledge of his will through all the wisdom and understanding that the Spirit gives" (1:9b). He recognizes that praying for wisdom and discernment is essential if leaders are to be Spirit-led and have the necessary wisdom and insight to lead well.

Paul's own ability to be decisive is significantly enhanced by his capacity to be Spirit-led. The Holy Spirit directs Paul's missionary activity, beginning with the very first journey. When Paul and Barnabas are commissioned by the Antioch church, they are "sent on their way by the Holy Spirit" (Acts 13:4). The same sense of divine guidance will mark Paul's ministry and missionary journeys.

Leadership Lesson: **The importance of prayer in a leader's decision-making cannot be overstated.**

Through prayer, the Holy Spirit is able to quicken a leader's mind, enabling the leader to discover creative options, assess potential outcomes and consequences of intended actions, discover wisdom, and gain the faith and courage to act.

Opened and Closed Doors

There are times when divine providence helps a leader be decisive. An unusual opportunity may present itself, causing the leader to realize the importance of immediate action; or, a significant hindrance could prompt a pause for reflection and new consideration. One aspect of decisiveness is the ability to recognize when the door of opportunity is open and when it is shut.

"Opened doors" is a term often used in Paul's missionary endeavors. In Acts 14:27, Luke tells of Paul and Barnabas's report to the church in Antioch at the conclusion of the first missionary journey, and they recount how God "opened a door of faith to the Gentiles." Paul writes to the Corinthians of his plans to stay in Ephesus for a season "because a great door for effective work has opened to me" (1 Corinthians 16:9); and that in Troas he "found that the Lord had opened a door for me" (2 Corinthians 2:12). Paul asks the Colossians to "pray for us, too, that God may open a door for our message" (4:3).

Leadership Lesson: **There are times when God opens the door of opportunity.**

Such open doors will always be aligned with God's Word, will be accompanied by confirmation, and will require faith and obedience to walk through. Open doors often signify new beginnings and new opportunities for the accomplishment of the mission.

There are also times when God closes doors for Paul. In Acts 16:6–7, Luke recounts that Paul and his companions are "kept by the Holy Spirit from preaching the word in the province of Asia. When they came to the border of Mysia, they tried to enter Bithynia, but the Spirit of Jesus would not allow them to." In this case, direction is provided mainly by prohibition. The Spirit shuts all the doors along the route. At Troas, Paul discovers that the reason the door has been closed to Asia and Bithynia is that another door is opening—the door to Macedonia (see vv. 9–10).

Leadership Lesson: Closed doors are just as valuable as open doors.

Sometimes circumstances clearly dictate that a proposed action will not or cannot take place, or is ill advised. If you are genuinely in doubt as to your course, ask the Spirit to close every door but the right one. In the meantime, continue along the course you have chosen; stay with the calling you have been pursuing. Do not be surprised when closed doors are God's answer. God sees the mission much more clearly than we do, and his plans for the accomplishment of his will sometimes result in the elimination of options.

Timely Action

Even when leaders have discernment and are able to recognize open and closed doors, they still need courage to act in a timely manner. There is seldom enough data or information to guarantee that any given decision is correct. Almost always, only *after* a decision is made can it be determined whether the decision was right.

Leadership Lesson: Don't let "analysis paralysis" keep you from making good decisions.

The leader must be able to act in a timely fashion, which often takes courage. Fear of making a mistake is one of the most common reasons that leaders are unable to move forward with decisions. Too many leaders get caught up in analysis paralysis, which plays out in the form of incessant information-gathering, unnecessarily prolonging the decision-making process. The ability to make decisions and continually move forward even when there is a lack of clarity is a critical leadership competency. No amount of data, reports, or forecasting projections will make the decision for you. At some point, a leader has to make the decision, even though the leader may never be one-hundred-percent certain that the decision is correct. Not every decision made will be correct, so another aspect of courage is to identify and rectify poor decisions. The natural tendency of those making decisions is to defend them, but taking too long to recognize a poor decision can negate a leader's effectiveness. Once a decision is made, it must be implemented. The importance of execution should not be missed. Good decisions that fail to be implemented become lost opportunities.

It is difficult to follow leaders who do not know where they are going. Paul is not guilty of either vacillation or unreliability. This truth is especially evident as Paul marches toward Jerusalem at the conclusion of his third missionary journey. In Acts 21, numerous people attempt to dissuade Paul from continuing, but he is resolute and unflinching. Paul determines to press on, even when Agabus comes from Judea and prophesies Paul's capture in Jerusalem (see Acts 21:10–15).

Being decisive doesn't have to mean being arrogant, stubborn, or hasty; it simply means having the ability to make decisions with clarity. Some people try to escape the possibility of failure by avoiding making difficult decisions, but that is not helpful. The ability to be decisive is a critical element of leadership success.

Leadership Lesson: **Vacillation in leaders creates confusion in followers.**

Good leaders must be able to make decisions that are clear-headed, proactive, and conclusive. Learning to be decisive is an essential skill that will increase any leader's effectiveness.

Questions for Leadership Development

1. What does your typical decision-making process look like?

2. How often do you pray for wisdom and revelation when making decisions?

3. Has the Holy Spirit been more likely to close doors or open doors in your life?

4. How do you discern that God is opening or closing a door? Have you ever tried to force open a door that the Holy Spirit closed?

5. How does a leader avoid analysis paralysis and become more decisive?

— NINETEEN —

COMMUNICATIVE

For we do not write you anything you cannot read or understand.
—2 Corinthians 1:13a

In any leadership position, the ability to communicate clearly and effectively, whether in public speaking or correspondence, is an important competency. Communication is how leaders cast vision, build teams, give direction, motivate people, provide correction, and inspire action. Paul's communication skills are significant. He is at least trilingual—able to communicate in Hebrew, Aramaic, and Greek—and his writing abilities are superb.

Paul's primary communication tool in starting churches is preaching. His primary communication tool in strengthening churches is writing. And his primary communication tool in developing leaders is one-on-one mentorship.

Starting Churches: Preaching

Immediately after his conversion, Paul begins to preach. Beginning in Damascus, "At once he began to preach in the synagogues that Jesus is the Son of God" (Acts 9:20).

Paul has a lot to say about preaching—so much so that he mentions it at least forty-five times in his letters, and Luke references Paul's preaching at least sixteen times. In 1 Corinthians 9:16, Paul writes of his mandate: "For when I preach the gospel, I cannot boast, since I am compelled to preach. Woe to me if I do not preach the gospel!" He also clearly defines his message: "But we preach Christ crucified: a stumbling block to Jews and foolishness to Gentiles, but to those whom God has called, both Jews and Greeks, Christ the power of God and the wisdom of God" (1 Corinthians 1:23–24).

Paul's preaching is biblically grounded (see Acts 17:11), gospel-centered (v. 18), culturally relevant (vv. 21–23), and persuasive (v. 4). For Paul, preaching is a priority. In Acts 18:5, Luke writes that, after the arrival of Silas and Timothy to Corinth, Paul "devoted himself exclusively to preaching, testifying to the Jews that Jesus was the Messiah." Through his preaching, Paul wins converts and then disciples them. As a result, churches are established.

Paul's preaching always begins where his hearers are. He preaches the gospel differently in Acts 13 (to "fellow children of Abraham and God-fearing Gentiles," v. 26) than in Acts 14 (to polytheistic pagans, see vv. 11–18) than in Acts 17 (to philosophers, see v. 18). In Antioch in Pisidia, Paul is preaching in a synagogue to Jews, proselytes, and God-fearers. He therefore begins with Jewish history and uses the Old Testament to prove his case (see 13:14–52). When Paul preaches in Athens, he creates rapport and uses language that connects with his hearers. He doesn't expressly quote Old Testament passages, which are unknown to his hearers. Instead, he quotes Greek poets—touchstones for the audience (see 17:28). Paul's approach is flexible. He begins where his audience is.

While Paul's sermons *begin* where the hearers are, they always *end* with Jesus Christ. In Thessalonica, for example, Paul "reasoned with them from the Scriptures, explaining and proving that the Messiah had to suffer and rise from the dead. 'This Jesus I am proclaiming to you is the Messiah,' he said" (17:2b–3).

Leadership Lesson: **Preaching that begins where the hearers are and ends with Christ is most effective.**

An awareness of audience context and culture allows a preacher to connect with the hearers. Preaching Jesus Christ provides an opportunity for the Holy Spirit to connect with the hearers.

Strengthening Churches: Writing

We know more about Paul's writing than we know of his preaching. Paul strengthens churches by writing letters that will ensure the continuation of his ministry influence and by developing leaders to serve them well. Paul's letters become substitutes for his personal presence and are written to encourage, instruct, correct, and rebuke. J. Oswald Sanders observes of Paul, "When he had a difficult letter to write, he was careful to dip his pen in tears and not in acid."[1]

At the end of his letter to the Galatians, it seems that Paul takes the pen from his amanuensis (the person who has been taking the dictation and transcribing the letter for him) and writes something more than his usual brief paragraph. He asks the recipients to excuse the clumsy handwriting and take note of how much larger his penmanship is than his assistant's. F. B. Meyer notes that Paul's words here can be taken in a metaphorical sense.[2] Paul's letters *are* large! They make up a quarter of the New Testament, not the least of which include:

- The sublime chapter on love (1 Corinthians 13)
- The matchless argument for justification (Romans 4–5)
- The inspiration to be overcoming conquerors (Romans 8)
- The wonderful hope of resurrection (1 Corinthians 15)
- Beautiful christological hymns (Philippians 2; Colossians 1)
- The classic passage on spiritual warfare (Ephesians 6:10–18)

We will consider a brief overview of Paul's letters in the order they appear in the New Testament.

Romans

Written from Corinth, Romans is the longest and most complex of Paul's letters.

He writes it for theological, pastoral, and missional reasons. Paul is teaching doctrine (theological); trying to settle the controversy between the Jewish Christians and the gentile Christians over the issue of meat sacrificed to idols (pastoral); and trying to establish Rome as the launching point for missionary efforts to Spain (missional), much like Antioch has been for his other journeys.

1 and 2 Corinthians

Paul spends eighteen months in Corinth, and by the time he leaves, there is a large and vigorous—though volatile—church established there. His time in Corinth "deepened his human sympathy and promoted his pastoral maturity."[3]

First Corinthians is written toward the end of Paul's three years in Ephesus, when Apollos and members of the house of Chloe bring an unsettling report from Corinth. A parade of problems has arisen, and 1 Corinthians is written to address them. The Corinthians are quick to believe but apparently slow to mature. The church is divided into factions, seriously threatening the unity of the church. False teachers have come to town and are taking advantage of the leadership vacuum. The new converts are at a point of yielding to the sensuous influences of the city. "The right attitude toward sex was inevitably a burning question to Corinthian Christians. Paul was so sure that misuse of sex damaged human personality, flouted divine law, and invited inevitable misery, that he could not let his converts adapt their ethics to the situation in which they were placed."[4]

After writing 1 Corinthians, Paul leaves Ephesus, where he is ministering, and makes a quick, disastrous visit to Corinth to address the issues that have arisen. He is humiliated in public in what becomes a deeply sorrowful memory (see 2 Corinthians 2:1). Apparently, one or more of the Corinthian leaders oppose Paul to his face with insults and mockery. His authority is resisted and rebuffed, his exit necessarily hasty. The deterioration of relations with the Corinthians church shatters Paul's confidence.

The corrective Paul of 1 Corinthians becomes the crushed Paul of 2 Corinthians.

No epistle reveals Paul's heart more than this second letter to the believers in Corinth. It is the most personal and passionate of all of Paul's canonized communications. It contains a depth of emotion and reveals a vulnerable, transparent soul. In chapter 4 he writes, "We are hard pressed on every side, but not crushed; perplexed, but not in despair; persecuted, but not abandoned; struck down, but not destroyed" (vv. 8–9).

Leadership Lesson: **Authentic leaders disclose truthfully and appropriately, without manipulation or masks.**

They own up to fragility, pain, and their need for help from others. Leaders are often marked by cautious disclosure and limited transparency, sensing that the information they share about their struggles, pain, and insecurities might be used against them in the future. Paul's example is valuable. He is transparent with them, giving them a glimpse into his own pain and anguish over their dispute. His authenticity and genuineness win the Corinthians over and reestablish his credibility. Paul's transparency and pain leave them with hope. Even though the times are challenging, his faith is strong and unwavering. Authority can actually go up, not down, when a leader displays genuine vulnerability.

Galatians

Paul's visit to Galatia in his first missionary journey meets with great success. The people are affectionate and receptive. When Paul leaves Galatia, he travels to Corinth and stays there three months. During that time, he hears news of the fickleness of the Galatians. Proselytizers have infiltrated the converts, disparaging Paul's apostleship and authority and insisting on submission to Levitical law. Filled with righteous indignation, Paul calls the Galatians to freedom.

Paul's position on the circumcision issue is clear-cut: circumcision is not to be imposed on gentile Christians. The majority of the Galatian converts are former pagans who have never lived under Jewish law. The main danger to the Galatian churches is exchanging Christian freedom for legal bondage.

Galatians is the only one of Paul's letters not addressed to a person or a particular city but to an entire region (the central part of modern Turkey). It is an example of Paul's willingness to tackle a difficult situation.

Leadership Lesson: There are times when a leader must engage in tough conversations and address difficult situations directly.

To not do so would be dereliction of duty. The ability to challenge people while being empathetic to their personal circumstances is a key competency in leadership.

Ephesians

Paul writes Ephesians while imprisoned in Rome. In this letter, Paul unpacks a doctrine of the Holy Spirit and considers the implications of the church being the body of Christ. The uniqueness of this letter is the relational component, showing how the relationships of husband-wife, parent-child, and master-slave all point to the relationship between Christ and the church.

Philippians

Philippi is, for Paul, perhaps the brightest spot on the earth. His letter to the Philippians is filled with tender love for cherished friends. Epaphroditus has brought gifts of love from Philippi and returns with a joyful letter of love and gratitude. It is the happiest and most upbeat of Paul's letters, even though it is written while Paul languishes in prison. The letter is filled with joy, praise for Christ, and gratitude for the amazing generosity of the Philippians.

Colossians

Paul writes Colossians toward the end of his first imprisonment in Rome. Epaphras, from Colossae, visits the apostle with news of a strange heresy spreading that calls the deity of Jesus Christ into question. In Colossians, Paul unfolds the cosmic role of Christ, describing Jesus with some of the loftiest language in the New Testament and focusing on Christ's preeminence and sufficiency.

1 and 2 Thessalonians

Paul founded the church in Thessalonica, but circumstances beyond his control forced him to leave the city before the converts were firmly established. First Thessalonians, likely the first letter Paul ever writes, is occasioned by Paul's relief at hearing the report from Timothy that the church is holding fast in the face of persecution. Paul is proud of them and writes to encourage them regarding the return of Jesus.

In 2 Thessalonians, the question of when Jesus will return and what that event will look like is the main focus. Paul writes to assure them that Jesus is Lord.

1 and 2 Timothy

Paul writes these letters to direct the young pastor assigned to Ephesus how to serve the church under his care. The letters are filled with pastoral advice and practical counsel. First Timothy is about sound doctrine and godliness. In 2 Timothy, Paul uses the examples of a good soldier, a trained athlete, and a hardworking farmer to show the need to endure hardships in order to lead well.

Titus

Written to the pastor Paul has assigned to Crete, the letter expounds the importance of sound doctrine and faithful elders.

Philemon

When Philemon—a landowner and slaveholder from Colossae—comes to Ephesus on business, he meets Paul and is converted. Philemon has a runaway slave named Onesimus, who also becomes a convert. Paul sends Onesimus back to his master with a letter that is "a perfect model of Christian courtesy."[5] Onesimus returns to serve, and Paul encourages Philemon to receive him in love, since one who was formerly "useless" is now "useful" (1:11). Philemon is the only one of Paul's letters that deals solely with a personal matter.

Leadership Lesson: Leaders who write—whether blogs, books, memoirs, articles, or even memos—have an opportunity to expand the breadth of their influence.

Leaders can communicate strategically in ways that shape, correct, guide, and clarify. Paul shows us how effective communication can be when leaders are contextual and intentional.

Developing Leaders: Mentorship

Although Paul preaches the gospel everywhere he goes and plants numerous churches, perhaps his most important contribution is discipling and developing leaders to join him in the mission. Paul's everyday interactions with those he disciples and mentors are not recorded, but we know they occur, and it is easy to imagine how: on ships, along the road as they travel from city to city, and sitting beside the loom of his tent-making business.

Crucial conversations happen with emerging leaders such as Timothy and Titus. Having trained and mentored them, Paul trusts them to lead effectively in challenging ministry assignments. Timothy and Titus serve as Paul's apostolic representatives, assigned to different locations so they can provide leadership in those respective churches. They are just two of dozens, if not hundreds, of leaders Paul invests in through everyday mentorship and leading by example, whose service strengthens the churches Paul plants.

Leadership Lesson: If, like Paul, you want to be a leader who develops leaders, find ways to encourage and invest in others through frequent, meaningful conversations.

Leaders are best developed through a combination of intentional training and informal, everyday interactions about life and leadership.

Questions for Leadership Development

1. When might it be advisable for a leader to be vulnerably transparent, and when would it not?

2. How does the culture of an organization make it easier or harder for leaders to be transparent?

3. Which mode of communication is most important to leadership—public speaking, written correspondence, or everyday interactions?

4. Can you name a Paul figure in your life who has invested in your spiritual development as well as your leadership development?

PART 5

THE LEADER'S CHALLENGES

What Makes Leaders Want to Quit?
Why Do Leaders Stay?

*Therefore, since through God's mercy we have this ministry,
we do not lose heart.*

*We are hard pressed on every side, but not crushed; perplexed,
but not in despair; persecuted, but not abandoned;
struck down, but not destroyed.*

*Therefore we do not lose heart. Though outwardly we are
wasting away, yet inwardly we are being renewed day by day.*
—2 Corinthians 4:1, 8–9, 16

*Are these challenges, or opportunities? If you are leading anything
more than yourself and find yourself without criticism, conflict, or
crisis, the most likely explanation is that you are not leading.*
—Joe McLamb[1]

In this last section on Paul's leadership, we will consider three challenges Paul faces. Criticism, conflict, and crises are weighty challenges that leaders often encounter. Paul demonstrates an ability to survive in the face of harsh personal adversity and to bounce back from failure and resistance.

Paul exhibits all the marks of resilient leadership—notably the ability to "stay calm, stay connected, and stay the course."[2] Tod Bolsinger suggests that challenges to leadership often result in two general breakdowns: failure of nerve and failure of heart. "Failure of nerve is caving to the pressure of the anxiety of the group to return to the status quo. It is a loss of courage to advance the mission. Failure of heart is when the leader's discouragement leads them to psychologically abandon their people and the charge they have been given."[3] A failure of nerve occurs when leaders are overcome by anxiety and surrender to the pressure of the resistance. A failure of heart occurs when leaders forsake the connection with those they serve and lose hope, energy, and passion.

The things that cause leaders to suffer a failure of nerve or a failure of heart are challenges like criticism, conflict, and crisis.

TWENTY

CRITICISM

*For some say, "His letters are weighty and forceful,
but in person he is unimpressive and
his speaking amounts to nothing."*
—2 Corinthians 10:10

The Impact of Criticism

Criticism is the act of finding fault, making negative observations, and passing severe judgment. We admire Paul for his strength in trials. We applaud his fierce determination against vicious persecution. Paul is beaten, lost at sea, stoned, flogged, and imprisoned. But what appears to most debilitate Paul is criticism. The emotional pain caused by criticism appears to hurt him more than even the significant physical pain he experiences in the fulfillment of the mission.

Leadership Lesson: Criticism is seldom offered lovingly and graciously.

More often than not, criticism is shared anonymously and judgmentally. Charles Swindoll offers the "four spiritual flaws" of criticism:

1. Criticism always comes when we least need it.
2. Criticism seems to come when we least deserve it.
3. Criticism comes from people least qualified to give it.
4. Criticism frequently comes in a form that is least helpful to us.[1]

When offered lovingly and graciously, what might otherwise be criticism becomes leadership development, coaching, or mentoring.

Criticism at Corinth

If anyone has reason to be snarky, it is the apostle Paul. But he is not sarcastic in his response to criticism. In fact, when addressing his detractors in Corinth, his response is marked by grace: "By the humility and gentleness of Christ, I appeal to you" (2 Corinthians 10:1a).

Leadership Lesson: **When we face criticism and conflict, our actions and character will speak louder than words.**

Critics are never in short supply, to put it mildly. The best way we can maintain our composure is through prayer, the encouragement of Scripture, the support of friends, and the power of the Holy Spirit. Paul reminds us that our battle is spiritual, not a battle with other people, and we have to fight accordingly (see 2 Corinthians 10:3–4).

In 2 Corinthians, Paul is responding to criticisms that have come in four areas: the way Paul looks, the way he speaks, the way he leads, and his status as an apostle. The critics have apparently claimed that Paul is homely, a lousy preacher, and lacking charisma and credibility.

Paul addresses the criticism against his physical appearance by humbly acknowledging his own deficiencies. In 2 Corinthians 10:10, Paul quotes some of the things that have been said—that he is not a physically imposing person, that his speech is unimpressive. He honestly and humbly acknowledges his own insufficiency and turns the tables on his accusers by agreeing with their claims. He chooses, instead, to "boast all the more gladly about my weaknesses, so that Christ's power may rest on me" (2 Corinthians 12:9).

He acknowledges that everything said about his physical infirmities is true, then quickly adds that it isn't about *him*. He is simply an ordinary, blemished clay pot that God has decided to use. The more fragile the vessel, the more evident it will be that God's power is at work and not human ability. Paul delights in the contrast between the majesty of the message and the insignificance of the messenger. He accepts his affliction with humility.

It is clear that the Corinthians place a great deal of importance on oratorical skill. In Paul's judgment, however, his *knowledge* more than compensates for any perceived lack. Paul defends himself with the argument that his weaknesses, coupled with the results of his ministry in Corinth, point to the power of God at work through him.

Leadership Lesson: Weaknesses need not be obstacles to leadership.

All leaders are beset with blemishes. An honest assessment and acknowledgment of deficiencies can help leaders get out of the way and allow God to shine through. Paul draws strength from remembering his own weakness. He knows he is inadequate on his own. The source of his adequacy is God. In much the same way that Moses's infirmity (his voice) makes him exactly the leader God and Israel need, so Paul's weakness makes him exactly the leader God and the church need.[2] God always uses human inadequacy and weakness. Once we recognize how desperately we need Jesus, he supplies what is lacking in our lives.

In 2 Corinthians 11 and 12, Paul defends himself against criticism and makes a case for his ministry as an apostle. It rankles some of the "super-apostles" that Paul, unlike his rivals, preaches the gospel of God "free of charge" (11:5, 7). One can easily see why Paul's policy of waiving support would cause his rivals consternation. While the super-apostles assert that such support is a sign of apostolic legitimacy, the fact remains that they are a financial burden and he is not. Paul resolutely refuses to abandon his policy of offering the gospel free of charge: "I have kept myself from being a burden to you in any way, and will continue to do so" (11:9b).

The detractors claim that Paul's volunteer status constitutes an admission that he is a second-rate apostle. Paul categorically denies this accusation and makes it plain to the Corinthians that he waived support so as not to hinder reception of the gospel message. It is his policy not to accept support from the church at which he is currently ministering. He reminds the Corinthian believers that his previous sufferings are marks of his apostleship (see 11:16–33).

Leadership Lesson: It is important for leaders to determine the nature of the criticism being received.

There are at least four different sources of criticism:

- Negative observations made by people who lack context. Sometimes criticism comes from the ill-informed. This type of criticism should not be taken to heart.
- Negative observations made by people who are truly aware. These criticisms can be constructive if the leader has the capacity to learn from them and adapt. When someone whom you know cares about you criticizes you, the best response is simply, "Thank you."
- Negative observations made by people who are jealous. Look for any kernel of truth in the criticism that may need to be acknowledged; disregard the rest.
- Negative observations made by people who want to sabotage your ministry. This type is what Paul is combating in 2 Corinthians 10–11, and he does so humbly, directly, and effectively.

Criticism before Felix in Acts 24

Toward the end of his third missionary journey, Paul's critics dog his steps from Antioch to Macedonia to Jerusalem. They are relentless. After a narrow escape from an ambush in Jerusalem, Paul is escorted to Caesarea by a protective detail of Roman soldiers. In Caesarea, Paul encounters "a trio of the state's more beguiling characters—Felix, Festus, and Agrippa—a motley group of governors, pompous in their outward displays, but weak in character and prejudiced in their dealing with anyone who was Jewish."[3]

In Acts 24, Paul finds himself before Felix, responding to the charges that have been levied by the Jewish critics—that Paul is a troublemaker and a desecrater of the temple. Swindoll suggests that Paul's response to the negative criticism provides a primer for leaders facing disparagement:

- He graciously acknowledges the opportunity to respond to the charges.
- He refuses to get caught up in the emotion of the criticism.
- He states the facts, telling the truth with a clear conscience. He doesn't exaggerate, and he doesn't avoid the part of the truth that doesn't bolster his argument. His integrity gives him personal credibility.
- He identifies the original source of the conflict.
- He does not become impatient or bitter.
- He does not surrender or quit.[4]

Leadership Lesson: **Criticism can be an inconsequential nuisance, a crushing burden, a constructive observation, or a dangerous threat.**

Being misrepresented, slandered, and wrongly accused are unfortunately often inevitable aspects of leadership. Leadership will always generate criticism. Perhaps the best defense against criticism is to cultivate thick skin and a tender heart. The opposite—having a tough heart and thin skin—makes it difficult to deal with criticism in a beneficial way. When criticized, don't quit.

Questions for Leadership Development

1. To which temptation—failure of nerve or failure of heart—are you most susceptible?

2. Reflect on your own weaknesses. How has God redeemed them?

3. Think back to the last time you heard from a critic. How did you respond? What is one way you could have handled it better?

4. When you find yourself in the position of critic, how do you express your criticism?

— TWENTY-ONE —

CONFLICT

For when we came into Macedonia, we had no rest,
but we were harassed at every turn—
conflicts on the outside, fears within.
—2 Corinthians 7:5

A second significant challenge Paul faces is conflict. Conflict can range from mild disagreement to violent altercation. Paul experiences both extremes and everything in between.

Leadership Lesson: **Because it emerges when there are differing viewpoints, leaders will inevitably face conflict.**

Conflict is a byproduct of community. The skills to recognize and identify the underlying cause(s) of the conflict and discern how to address it in a beneficial way become critical to conflict resolution. Leaders need both rain and sunshine to grow, but the rain produced by a shower is more beneficial than a typhoon. In the same way, the inconvenience produced by a minor conflict can prompt beneficial change, while the devastation produced by a major conflict may well doom both leader and organization. Conflict can provide an opportunity to make things better. Keeping minor conflict from becoming major is key to effective leadership and healthy organizations.

Physical Conflict

Paul, in his travels, often experiences violent altercations. He shares a list of the worst of it in 2 Corinthians: "Five times I received from the Jews the forty lashes minus one. Three times I was beaten with rods, once I was pelted with stones" (11:24–25a). We'll briefly explore three occasions when Paul is confronted with violence.

Damascus: A Basket Case (Acts 9:23–25)

Early in Paul's ministry, he has to be delivered from violence by his followers in Damascus. Immediately after his conversion, Paul begins to preach about Jesus in the Damascus synagogue. The Jews in the city—who expect Paul's arrival to have a chilling effect on the Damascus Christians—are frustrated when Paul's actions have the opposite effect. A conspiracy is hatched to assassinate Paul when he approaches the city gates. To avoid the danger, Paul's followers let him down over the city wall in a basket, and Paul escapes. This will not be the last time Paul's friends hustle him out of town when there are threats of violence against him.

Leadership Lesson: **When facing imminent danger, often the most prudent course of action is to find a way to avoid violence.**

If you are unable to deescalate the situation, the best option may be to remove yourself from the situation. Across the centuries, Christians have often fled persecution, which has done much to spread the gospel. Discerning when to confront violence and when to avoid it is key. By engaging in violence, a leader may be escalating danger, rather than ending it. At no point does Paul ever respond to violence with violence. When confronted with the possibility of violence, explore options for avoidance. Although it is seldom beneficial to ignore conflict, it is often useful to avoid it. There are times when we should take action to stop violence, especially if it is being perpetrated against the weak or innocent. A leader need not engage every conflict, however. This guideline also has implications for social media, where people often make war with their words. Explore other options, including disengagement. In Paul's case, violence is usually either avoided or endured. Fortunately for him, there are instances when others intercede.

Ephesus: A Riot (Acts 19:23–41)

It has been suggested that Paul's arrival in a city either results in a revival or a riot. In Ephesus, both occur. The success of Paul's evangelistic activity impacts the number of worshipers of the goddess Artemis, which in turn impacts the income of those who depend on the Artemis cult for their sales. The local silversmiths' guild, led by Demetrius, has the same problem with Paul as the slave owners in Philippi: their livelihood is threatened by Paul's preaching.

Leadership Lesson: **If your leadership has a negative impact on someone's ill-gotten gain, expect strong opposition.**

While many are blessed as a result of Paul's preaching, the silversmiths' income is negatively affected. Most every cultural change positively impacts some and negatively impacts others. Purveyors of evil are always negatively impacted by revival, thus resistance and significant pushback often result.

Demetrius inflames the mob. They lay hands on two of Paul's companions—Gaius and Aristarchus—and drag them into the theater. Paul wants to address the mob, but friends restrain him. The city secretary, thoroughly alarmed, quiets the crowd and warns them of the likely serious consequences of their riot, and the mob disperses.

Leadership Lesson: **Sometimes the intercession of others delivers us from the threat of violence.**

Thank God for friends who offer wise counsel and for responsible leaders who deescalate volatile situations. It is a terrible thing to have aggressive enemies and passive friends.[1] Fortunately for Paul, his friends are as resolute as his enemies.

Lystra: A Stone's Throw from Death (Acts 14:8–20)

Though they are greeted enthusiastically at first and even lauded as gods, public opinion at Lystra soon turns against Paul and Barnabas. When troublemakers from Pisidian Antioch and Iconium arrive, the crowd is stirred to violence, and Paul takes the brunt of it. Unable to flee, he is stoned until knocked unconscious; he is literally one more stone's throw from death's door. Those who stoned him "dragged him outside the city, thinking he was dead" (v. 19). Paul's ill treatment at Lystra likely results in permanent scars.

Leadership Lesson: **A tough and resilient constitution will serve a leader well.**

Paul has remarkable staying power—"often knocked down but never knocked out"—as 2 Corinthians 4:9 is often paraphrased. One wonders if Paul remembers the impact of Stephen's response to his persecution and hopes that his own response will bear similar fruit.

Emotional Conflict

Disappointment falls into the gap between expectation and reality. The gap between the reality of John Mark's desertion early in Paul's first missionary journey and the expectation that he will be a contributing team member for the duration of the trip results in great disappointment for Paul. So, when Barnabas suggests that John Mark accompany them on their next journey, Paul has no desire to experience that disappointment again. The ensuing conflict results in the separation and estrangement of two close friends.

Leadership Lesson: Godly, spiritual leaders sometimes find themselves in conflict with other godly, spiritual leaders.

Chuck Swindoll suggests some important considerations that may save the day when we find ourselves in sharp disagreement with a colleague:

- When in disagreement, work hard to see the other point of view. This means listening well. Paul advises that the people of God "value others above yourselves, not looking to your own interests but each of you to the interests of the others" (Philippians 2:3b–4). Disagreement takes place when an issue is seen from two opposing points of view. Resolution becomes possible when each side is willing to consider the other point of view.

- When both sides have validity, seek a wise compromise. Seek a suitable solution that honors the truth in both sides of the disagreement. Paul could choose a probationary period. Barnabas could agree to an intermediate step. They both could opt for a contingency plan.

- If you are compelled to differ from your companions, let it be in love. When the conflict cannot be resolved, graciously agree to disagree without becoming disagreeable. As Abraham demonstrates, if Lot quarrels with you, it is better to give him his own terms and send him away (see Genesis 13:8–9).

- When the conflict persists, care enough to work through it rather than walk out. Don't bolt or quit in a huff. Stay engaged with your friend, lest they become your former friend.[2]

Providentially, sometimes leadership squabbles result in two fruitful teams instead of one. Paul and Barnabas's conflict will result in a doubling of the missionary force. While the cause of the disagreement is unfortunate and the lack of resolution disappointing, the ultimate result of the conflict will be an increase in ministry impact.

Paul has other disappointing relationships, some of which he refers to in 2 Timothy 4:9–16. He wants Timothy to be aware of those he can rely on and those who may prove undependable. Several have caused Paul intense grief. Demas has forsaken Paul and departed for Thessalonica, leaving Paul in the lurch. The treachery of Alexander the coppersmith has done Paul much harm, and Timothy should beware. There are also several other anonymous deserters.

Leadership Lesson; If you lead long enough, you will suffer the desertion of a key leader and be disappointed by a close friend.

When rejected or disappointed, don't quit. Instead, resolve to be grateful for the coworkers who have remained faithful, and covenant with yourself to be a friend others can count on, even when it costs something.

Theological Conflict

Antioch will become the launching point of a movement, but it will also be the focal point of a theological conflict. Male gentiles converting to Judaism are required to submit to circumcision. In Antioch, the question arises about whether gentile converts to Christianity must also be circumcised. Jewish Christians who regard the Levitical laws as still binding for all Christians come from Jerusalem to Antioch and disturb the church by demanding that the gentile converts to Christianity be circumcised.

When Paul and Barnabas report back following the first missionary journey, the church in Antioch is thrilled. The news is not received with such elation in Jerusalem. The Jerusalem leaders did not anticipate such a large influx of gentile believers. With such an increase, the gentiles will soon outnumber the Jewish Christians. How are the church's ethical standards to be safeguarded? Some members of the Jerusalem church propose a simple solution: gentile converts to Christianity should comply with the same requirements as gentile converts to Judaism, so men should be circumcised, and all believers should keep the Law of Moses. Some of these people visit Antioch and try to impose this line of thinking: "Unless you are circumcised, according to the custom taught by Moses, you cannot be saved" (Acts 15:1).

If only the gentiles who believe in Jesus will become circumcised, everyone will be happy! From the perspective of the folks from Jerusalem, this solution makes sense. From Paul's perspective, it makes no sense. Forcing gentiles to become Jewish in order to become Christian seems to Paul to seriously disfigure the gospel message.

Leadership Lesson: Even in times of significant growth and fruitfulness, leadership challenges will be lurking.

Such is the case at Antioch. The church is growing, and leaders are emerging and being developed. But a significant issue arises that threatens the church in Antioch, and in every other location where gentiles are coming to faith in Jesus. Good leaders are able to recognize challenges early and address them. One component of addressing challenges effectively is to identify the person or group with the ultimate decision-making authority to resolve the challenge.

As the controversy continues, the Antioch church sends Paul, Barnabas, and several others to Jerusalem to finally settle the question about circumcision. The meeting of the Jerusalem Council described by Luke in Acts 15 is a meeting of the leaders of the Jerusalem church to settle this issue. The council declares that circumcision is not necessary for gentile converts—a decision that must please Paul and the church at Antioch a great deal—but it does not mean there are no expectations. There are certain requirements the gentile believers are to observe.

First, three requirements of food restriction are presented. These are practical concessions for gentiles that will make table fellowship possible for Jewish Christians. Gentile believers are to abstain from eating the flesh of animals that have been sacrificed to pagan deities, meat from strangled animals, and flesh from which the blood has not been completely drained. Second, they are to abstain from fornication. Sexual immorality is incompatible with the Christian way. Paul will be clear that those who persist in this kind of practice must not be tolerated in the church.

The conference ends amicably with the understanding that Paul and Barnabas will minister in the gentile territories while the others work in Israel. The council's decisions are endorsed by all, and the conclusion is sent to Antioch by letter.

Leadership Lesson: God makes his will known through his Word, the gentle nudging of the Spirit, and the collective witness of God's people.[3]

The Jerusalem Council, through prayerful consideration, will be led by the Spirit to a decision that will bless and guide the church. All such decision-making bodies will benefit from a similar approach—prayerfully studying the Word, responding to the leading of the Spirit, and seeking a unifying resolution.

Although the issue is officially resolved by the Jerusalem Council, it continues to be a recurring issue in other places—notably Galatia—and will dog Paul's ministry for years to come. False teachers come to Galatia as soon as Paul leaves. Paul's leadership is directly attacked, and his opponents see some success in making the circumcision issue into a controversy in Asia Minor. Paul addresses the threat directly in his letter to the Galatians.

Leadership Lesson: **The importance of following up to reduce the potential of confusion or growing conflict cannot be overstated.**

The Galatian trouble will show Paul that he needs to change his strategy. While his vision remains twofold—first, to win believers to Christ; second, to form churches that will endure without him and send out missionaries themselves until the world is covered for Christ—he recognizes the need to return soon to the young churches with a follow-up trip to check on progress and ensure they are not straying doctrinally or morally. After planting churches, Paul will be careful to revisit the fledgling faith communities. He will begin retracing his steps, checking on the progress of the newly planted churches, observing their direction to see if it needs correction, and encouraging them in the faith. Paul will also endeavor to stay in an epicenter longer, ensuring the converts are well established.

Questions for Leadership Development

1. What is your preferred approach in dealing with conflict?

2. What basic ground rules sustain you when conflict arises?

3. Does your organization/church have a shared understanding about the boundaries of appropriate behavior?

4. When is it best to choose avoidance or deescalation rather than confrontation and the threat of violence?

TWENTY-TWO

CRISIS

When neither sun nor stars appeared for many days
and the storm continued raging,
we finally gave up all hope of being saved.
—Acts 27:20

The third kind of challenge that Paul faces is crisis. A crisis is an extreme circumstance that jeopardizes the health and future of the leader and/or the organization. It is often a time marked by high anxiety and uncertainty and can lead to either a failure of nerve or a failure of heart.

There are plenty of situations in Paul's life that would qualify as crises. In many ways, Paul's entire ministry is composed of one crisis after another. Things we would consider extreme emergencies seem to happen to him on a regular basis: beatings, rejection, riots, and near-death experiences. In this chapter we will consider three incidents that are among the most dramatic in Paul's life.

Riot (Acts 21:17–26:32)

In Acts 21:11, the prophet Agabus warns Paul what awaits him in Jerusalem: he will be taken captive by the Jews and handed over to the gentiles. That is exactly what happens at the end of Paul's third missionary journey.

When Paul and the representatives of the gentile churches deliver the offering to the saints in Jerusalem, the elders suggest Paul pay the expenses and share the vigil of four poor men making a vow of purity. The elders believe this will dispel any questions about the credibility of Paul's ministry and prove he is not ignoring the law and teaching others to do the same. Paul agrees to the elders' plan. He joins the group, pays their expenses, follows the ritual, keeps the fast.

The danger comes suddenly, when Paul and the other men enter the temple after a week of purification. Some Jews from Asia observe Paul in the inner courts and accuse him of deliberately defiling the temple area. They know Paul has been traveling with Trophimus, and they falsely assume he has brought the gentile into the temple, which is forbidden. They start a riot that is born out of a misunderstanding but fueled by their hatred of Paul.

The surrounding crowd turns on Paul and drags him into the gentile courtyard, where they proceed to beat him, intent on killing him for polluting the temple. Paul would not survive the violent beating were it not for the timely arrival of the Roman garrison posted in the Antonian fortress. He is rescued by Lysias and the legionnaires, who respond to the disturbance immediately. Paul is arrested, but the noise of the crowd makes it impossible to question him, so they carry Paul back to their barracks.

Leadership Lesson: Assumptions—both our own and those of others—have great power to get leaders in trouble.

In this instance, as often occurs among a hostile crowd, a false rumor spreads like wildfire and is accepted as truth. When leaders are the victims of assumptions, it is best to make the truth known as soon as possible. When tempted to leap to conclusions themselves, it is best for leaders to carefully avoid assumptions and act on the basis of what is known to be reality.

When they reach the barracks, Paul asks to address the mob, and he shares with them the story of his conversion and call. When he mentions being sent to the gentiles, the crowd erupts again, and the commander orders that Paul be taken to the barracks and flogged. F. F. Bruce explains, "Both Greek and Roman legal systems had the idea that people were more likely to tell the truth under torture, or the threat of it, but Greek law generally exempted freemen from such treatment, and Roman law exempted Roman citizens."[1] As Paul is being tied up, he asks if it is permissible to scourge a Roman citizen, especially one against whom no crime has been proven in open court. Upon learning of Paul's citizenship, the commander releases him and has him appear before the Sanhedrin. Again, the crowd erupts in violence, and Paul has to be rescued and taken back to the barracks.

Paul's enemies, seeing that there is no legal way to get him into their hands, plot to kill him. Forty assassins take a vow to not eat or drink until they have taken Paul's life. Paul's nephew overhears the plot, and Paul encourages him to report it to the Roman commander. The commander orders that Paul be immediately transported to Caesarea for safekeeping by a protective detail of 472 soldiers.

Leadership Lesson: God's deliverance can come from unlikely sources.

A nephew and a Roman cohort become God's means of delivering Paul. God is always at work on behalf of God's people. Rarely has a leader had such an overwhelming protective detail as Paul does that night.

In the providence of God, leaders are often delivered from peril, both in ways we are aware, and perhaps in ways we are unaware.

Paul will be imprisoned for two years in Caesarea, the main Roman military outpost on the coast of Israel. He will appear before Felix, Festus, and Agrippa. When the high priest comes down from Jerusalem with a high-powered lawyer named Tertullus, Felix recognizes that the Jews have no case under Roman law and that Paul should be acquitted. But he delays releasing him, and Paul eventually appeals to Caesar—perhaps to remove himself from local prejudice, or to achieve his long-cherished dream to proclaim the gospel in Rome.

Storm (Acts 27:1–26)

Since Paul is a prisoner, he will be sent to Rome under the care of Julius, a centurion "who belonged to the Imperial Regiment" (27:1). Julius is likely assigned to work throughout the empire on escort duty. Paul is permitted to take two attendants, and he chooses Aristarchus and Luke. Sailing from Caesarea, the ship puts in for a day in Sidon, where Paul is allowed to go ashore to visit his friends.

Leadership Lesson: Those you assume to be your enemy are not always your enemy.

John MacArthur notes that "every time you encounter a Roman centurion in Scripture, you find a man of integrity—a respectable, intelligent, virtuous man."[2] We meet centurions in Matthew 8, Luke 7, Mark 15, Acts 10, Acts 22, and Acts 24, and all of them are upright men of decency and honor. Julius is no exception. A highly trained, seasoned commander, Julius lets his prisoner have freedom after being with him only one day.

The luxury is apparently permitted because Paul is a Roman citizen and has already gained Julius's favor.

At Myra, Julius transfers his prisoners and soldiers to a ship hauling grain from Egypt to Rome. By Roman practice, as representative of Rome, Julius will have the last word in any emergency. His party increases the complement of the ship to 276 souls, indicating a large ship. One can imagine crowded conditions.

At Fair Havens they put in and wait for the winds to change. Since the safe season for Mediterranean navigation is ending, they hold a ship's council while they wait. Paul is invited to participate, perhaps because he is an experienced traveler. He urges them to stay in Fair Havens, foreseeing danger and disaster if they continue. The pilot and ship owner think they should proceed to a more accommodating harbor. The centurion sides with them, and the decision is made. Soon thereafter, the wind changes, and they set sail. But as they follow the shore of Crete, the wind changes again. This time it is a Northeaster, a terrible storm that will rage for many days with hurricane-like winds.

Leadership Lesson: Contrary winds are the bane of leadership.

There are many circumstances that cannot be controlled, only responded to. There are days you feel the wind of the Spirit at your back, and things go smoothly. Then there are days when nothing works, the headwinds are strong, and the waves are high. The best option is to stay engaged and persevere. Every storm eventually runs out of rain.

It isn't unusual for passengers to grow nervous in foul weather, but when the crew gets panicky, that's truly cause for concern. Acts 27 reveals how the trouble progressively worsens:

- Verse 4: "The winds were against us."
- Verse 7: "We made slow headway for many days."
- Verse 8: "We moved along the coast with difficulty."
- Verse 9: "Much time had been lost."
- Verse 14: "A wind of hurricane force, called the Northeaster, swept down."
- Verse 18: "We took such a violent battering."
- Verse 20: "We finally gave up all hope of being saved."

What starts out as a forty-mile cruise along the coastline turns into several days of sheer, steadily increasing terror. Everything not nailed down—even the cargo—is thrown into the sea in a frantic effort to lighten the ship.

Leadership Lesson: In a crisis, you're probably going to have to sacrifice something.

In the midst of a storm, leaders need the ability to determine what is necessary and what is unnecessary, what must be kept at all costs and what can be jettisoned. Leaders must be willing to sacrifice—especially convenience, which is often the first thing to go.

Shipwreck (Acts 27:27–28:30)

The storm is raging, and the ship is floundering. After ten to twelve days of drifting, Paul has a vision. It is revealed to him that he will survive and that the lives of all his shipmates will be spared as well. But the ship will be lost.

Most of the people onboard with Paul have been seasick for several days. They have not eaten in some time, and wouldn't be able to keep it down if they had. The crew tries to secretly abandon ship. Everyone has lost hope. In this desperate situation, God speaks a word of encouragement to Paul, who becomes an agent of hope.

Paul's companions are on the verge of hopelessness when he exhorts them. *Keep up your courage! The ship's going down, but we're going to make it!*

Leadership Lesson: Courage in the leader inspires courage in the follower.

A leader inspires people to "take heart." A leader's confidence inspires courage in others, and Paul is able to give hope and encourage others to believe there will be a future. He speaks with boldness because his confidence originates from a strong sense of God's presence and guidance. He knows what is true. A leader strengthens others and keeps hope alive until help arrives. The interesting thing about Paul's voyage to Rome is how he takes charge. Paul is captain of neither ship nor guard, nor does he own the ship. He is a prisoner. But he is also a leader, and all aboard follow his lead. Leaders keep their heads when people are losing theirs all around. Paul shares with his shipmates the assurance that all will be saved. He urges them to eat something, knowing they will need strength to make it to shore.

Leadership Lesson: There are the three kinds of leaders in a crisis.

1. **Paralyzed leaders** suffer from a failure of nerve. The crisis freezes them. They may be in denial, disbelieving that the crisis is real, finding it difficult to act. Paralyzed leaders feel like they have no control. They can't adapt and are unable to see options. Some leaders, unwilling to make the necessary sacrifices, simply give up.

2. **Hesitant leaders** are tentative because they are afraid to fail. Hesitant leaders try to escape the possibility of disappointment by delaying difficult decisions and making as few changes as

possible. They take small, cautious steps when bold steps are needed.

3. **Adaptive leaders** are both flexible and courageous. They are willing to adapt methods to achieve the mission and sacrifice what is not essential. Adaptive leaders also continually ask questions to see what options might arise.

Finally, they run aground and abandon the ship as it breaks apart. The soldiers intend to kill the prisoners to prevent any escapes, but Julius forbids it. Amazingly, all 276 people reach land safely and are welcomed by the islanders. The people on Malta recognize that Paul and the others are cold, wet, and tired, and they welcome them by building a fire to provide heat and dry their clothing.

The islanders show "unusual kindness" (28:2) to the stranded castaways, in spite of the fact that many of the ship's passengers are prisoners and criminals. It seems like things are looking up. But, as Paul is helping gather sticks for the fire, a viper fastens itself on his hand. He has faced dangers from the storm, the sea, the soldiers—and now a snake.

Leadership Lesson: If you're in leadership long enough, you will be bitten by a snake (metaphorically or otherwise).

It's inevitable. You'll be betrayed by a friend you thought had your back. You'll be stunned by a person with evil intent. When leaders are bitten by snakes, people watch to see how they will respond. Will they become poisoned by the venom and filled with toxic bitterness? Will they swell up with resentment or pride? Paul's reaction is noteworthy. He shakes the snake off into the fire "and suffered no ill effects" (28:5). The natives expect Paul to puff up, poisoned by the toxin, and fall over dead. They think Paul is a murderer getting his just deserts. But Paul simply shakes the snake off into the fire, and when he doesn't swell up and die, the islanders change their opinion about him. His credibility escalates. What happens to us is not what usually does us in. It is our response to what happens to us that does us in. Good leaders don't just act like leaders; they also react like leaders. A snakebite can be fatal to your witness, to your credibility, to your usefulness, to your leadership—but it doesn't have to be. It depends on how you respond. The snakebite can become an open door for effective ministry. The very thing the enemy intends to take you out can give you a platform for greater influence to advance the kingdom of God. The snake—that which could have killed—becomes a testimony of God's grace, protection, and providence.

Unusual kindness leads to generous hospitality, and a door for effective ministry is opened when Publius, governor of the island, invites Paul and Luke into his home. Paul heals Publius's father and then every other sick person on the entire island. Today, two thousand years later, 96 percent of the inhabitants of Malta identify as Christian.[3] It all begins when Paul responds well to a snakebite.

The voyage to Rome is completed in the spring on another ship that wintered in Malta. In Rome, Paul is treated with great leniency. He will remain in custody in a house he rents at his own expense. Regulations demand the presence of a soldier, to whom he will be chained, but he is able to receive visitors and continue his ministry fairly unhindered. In the final words of Acts, Luke shares that Paul stays in Rome as a prisoner for two years at his own expense, preaching the Word of God "with all boldness and without hindrance!" (28:31).

We have no direct information about the outcome of Paul's first trial in Rome. Some scholars believe it ended with conviction and execution. Others think he was released, either through acquittal after trial, or because the case went against his accusers by default. Julius likely provided a character reference for Paul. If Paul's detention was followed immediately by his conviction and execution, Luke's failure to mention it is odd.

N. T. Wright suggests that perhaps Paul was released and made it to Spain, as Clement, a bishop in Spain, has insinuated.[4] Tradition associates Paul's execution with the persecution of Christians in Rome that followed the great fire of AD 64—at least two years after the date of his probable hearing. Nero accused the Christians of arson in an effort to divert suspicion from himself. Intense persecution broke out immediately, and Paul is assumed to have been arrested and hurried to Rome. He may have been singled out personally by Nero, since he had already appeared before him and since Paul was a well-known leader in the church.

Tradition points to the Mamertine prison as the scene of Paul's last weeks or months, and to a spot on the Ostian Road, about three miles from Rome, where Paul was beheaded with an axe.

One wonders whether, as the executioner's blade fell, Paul may have offered a smile to a young man standing nearby, holding the coat of the executioner.

Questions for Leadership Development

1. How do leaders ensure they are acting on facts and not assumptions?

2. What crises have you encountered in leadership?

3. What encourages you about your typical response in times of crisis?

4. What disappoints you about your typical response in times of crisis?

AFTERWORD
THE CHRISTLIKE LEADER

*I have been crucified with Christ and I no longer live,
but Christ lives in me. The life I now live in the body,
I live by faith in the Son of God, who loved me
and gave himself for me.*
—Galatians 2:20

*In the same way, count yourselves dead to sin
but alive to God in Christ Jesus.*
—Romans 6:11

What makes Paul a Christlike leader? It is easy to see how Paul's life and ministry are patterned after the life and ministry of Jesus. And the virtues exemplified in the life of Jesus are reflected in Paul's character. But perhaps what makes Paul a truly *Christlike* leader is that he enters into life *and* death with Jesus.

Paul is born in Tarsus. Several years later he is born again on the outskirts of Damascus. When he encounters the living Jesus, something is born anew within him. It is not he who lives, as he writes in Galatians 2:20, but Christ in him.

Paul never gets over his encounter with Jesus on the road to Damascus. His experience with Jesus Christ that day changes both the direction and the devotion of his life. Jesus, literally, becomes his life.

But Jesus brings not only life to Paul; Jesus also brings death to Paul. Long before Paul dies on the outskirts of Rome, he dies to sin and self-centeredness in his own life. "We are those who have died to sin," he reminds us in Romans 6:2; "how can we live in it any longer?" Paul is no longer the focus of his own life. No longer is he self-centered; now he is Jesus-centered.

Christ died so that Paul could truly live in him; Paul died so that Christ could truly live in him.

Leaders like Paul—who have experienced both a new birth and a death to sin and self-centeredness—will be used by God to change the world.

May you and I be such leaders—to the glory of God.

Questions for Leadership Development

1. Are you a leader who has been made alive in Jesus Christ?

2. Are you a leader who has died to sin and self-centeredness?

NOTES

Introduction: The C's of Leadership

1. Richard S. Ascough and Charles A. Cotton, *Passionate Visionary: Leadership Lessons from the Apostle Paul* (Peabody, MA: Hendrickson Publishers, 2006), 16.

2. Other leadership C's might include credibility, communication, commitment, confidence, creativity, collaboration, compassion, courage, and caring.

Part 1: The Leader's Call

1. Theodore Roosevelt, quoted in Doris Kearns Goodwin, *Leadership in Turbulent Times* (New York: Simon & Schuster, 2018), 158.

Chapter 1: Child of Tarsus: Before Leadership

1. F. B. Meyer, *Paul: A Servant of Jesus Christ* (Coppell, TX: Pantianos Classics, 2020), 11.

2. N. T. Wright, *Paul: A Biography* (New York: HarperCollins Publishers, 2018), 15.

3. Wright, *Paul*, 34.

4. Wright, *Paul*, 13.

5. I am indebted to Dean Flemming for this insight.

6. F. F. Bruce, *Paul: Apostle of the Heart Set Free* (Grand Rapids: Eerdmans, 2000), 37.

7. Meyer, *Paul*, 22.

8. Ascough and Cotton, *Passionate Visionary*, 24.

9. J. Oswald Sanders, *Paul the Leader* (Eastbourne, UK: Kingsway, 1983), 20.

10. I am indebted to Dean Flemming for this insight.

11. I am indebted to Josh Herndon for this insight.

Chapter 2: Child of Jerusalem: Education

1. Bruce, *Paul*, 126.

2. Wright, *Paul*, 34.

3. Meyer, *Paul*, 27.

4. J. D. Greear, "5 Lessons from the Life of Stephen," J. D. Greear Ministries (May 2014), https://jdgreear.com/5-lessons-from-the-life-of-stephen/.

5. Greear, "5 Lessons from the Life of Stephen."

Chapter 3: Child of Damascus: Transformation

1. Bruce, *Paul*, 72–73.

2. Augustine, quoted in Charles R. Swindoll, *Paul: A Man of Grace and Grit* (Nashville: Thomas Nelson, 2002), 22.

3. I am indebted to Joe McLamb for this insight.

4. Pope Benedict XVI, *Saint Paul* (Ignatius Press: San Francisco, 2017), 25.

5. Bruce, *Paul*, 75.

6. I am indebted to Tabita Gonzalez for this insight.

Chapter 4: Child of Arabia: Preparation

1. Wright, *Paul*, 63.

2. Wright, *Paul*, 72.

3. I am indebted to Dean Flemming for this insight.

4. The Hellenistic Jews were Jews who had adopted Greek language and culture, as opposed to Hebraic Jews, who held fast to Hebrew language and culture.

5. Swindoll, *Paul*, 79.

6. James Stalker, *The Life of Saint Paul* (New York: American Tract Society, 1884), 67.

7. I am indebted to Joe McLamb for this insight.

Chapter 5: Child of Antioch: Ordination

1. I am indebted to Joe McLamb for this insight.

2. Meyer, *Paul*, 68.

3. Bruce, *Paul*, 146.

4. I am indebted to Wayne Nelson for this insight.

5. Church of the Nazarene, *Manual: 2017–2021* (Kansas City, MO: Nazarene Publishing House, 2017), 192, paragraph 502.

6. I am indebted to Tabita Gonzalez for this insight.

7. Bruce, *Paul*, 148.

Part 2: The Leader's Connections

1. Widely attributed to Jon Katz without a specific source.

Chapter 6: First-Circle Connections: Traveling Companions

1. Tod Bolsinger, presentation to District Superintendent Leadership Development Program (DSLDP), Branson, MO (September 8, 2021).

2. The conflict between Paul and Barnabas will be explored in more depth in chapter 22.

3. Wright, *Paul*, 417.

Chapter 7: Second-Circle Connections: Ministry Colleagues

1. Bruce, *Paul*, 251.

2. A. T. Robinson, *Word Pictures in the New Testament, Vol. III: The Acts of the Apostles* (Nashville: Broadman Press, 1930), 241.

Chapter 8: Third-Circle Connections: Providential Contacts

1. Wright, *Paul*, 425.

Chapter 10: Resilient

1. I am indebted to Joe McLamb for this insight.

2. I am indebted to Scott Estep for this insight.

3. David Brooks, "What Do You Say to the Sufferer?" *New York Times* (December 2021), https://www.nytimes.com/2021/12/09/opinion/sufferer-stranger-pain.html.

4. Swindoll, *Paul*, 36.

5. John MacArthur, *Called to Lead: 26 Leadership Lessons from the Life of Paul* (Nashville: Thomas Nelson, 2004), 116.

6. Rick Atkinson, *The British Are Coming: The War for America, Lexington to Princeton, 1775–1777* (New York: Henry Holt and Company, 2019), 564.

Chapter 11: Compassionate

1. Wright, *Paul*, 257.

2. Bruce, *Paul*, 323.

3. Bruce, *Paul*, 461.

4. Bruce, *Paul*, 337.

Chapter 12: Self-Controlled

1. Barry J. Beitzel, *The Moody Atlas of Bible Lands* (Chicago: Moody Press, 1985), 176–77.

Chapter 13: Humble

1. Rick Warren, *The Purpose-Driven Life: What on Earth Am I Here for?* (Grand Rapids: Zondervan, 2002), 265.

2. Danielle Strickland, "True Humility," Global Leadership Network (May 2017), https://globalleadership.org/videos/leading-yourself/true-humility.

3. C. S. Lewis, *Mere Christianity* (New York: HarperCollins, 2000), 128.

4. Carey Nieuwhof, Twitter (March 28, 2022), https://twitter.com/cnieuwhof/status/1508368420215140354.

5. R. Scott Rodin, "Becoming a Leader of No Reputation," *Journal of Religious Leadership*, Vol. 1, No. 2 (Fall 2002), 106.

6. Henri J. M. Nouwen, *In the Name of Jesus: Reflections on Christian Leadership* (New York: Crossroads, 1966), 17.

7. MacArthur, *Called to Lead*, 103.

8. Rodin, "Becoming a Leader of No Reputation," 115.

9. Timothy Keller, Twitter (September 17, 2018), https://twitter.com/timkellernyc/status/1041750889277603840. Keller has repeated this statement verbatim and in other variations on Twitter on the following dates as well: January 20, 2021; January 23, 2018; July 10, 2016

10. Nouwen, *In the Name of Jesus*, 62–63.

11. Robert K. Greenleaf, "The Servant as Leader" (South Orange, NJ: Robert K. Greenleaf Center for Servant Leadership, 1970), 7.

12. Quoted in James O'Toole, *Leading Change: An Argument for Values-Based Leadership* (New York: Ballantine Books, 1995), 44.

13. Swindoll, *Paul*, 229.

Chapter 14: Missional

1. Alan Hirsch, *The Forgotten Ways: Reactivating the Missional Church* (Grand Rapids: Brazos Press, 2006).

2. Alan Hirsch and Tim Catchim, *The Permanent Revolution: Apostolic Imagination and Practice for the 21st-Century Church* (San Francisco: Jossey-Bass, 2012), 148.

3. Frederick Buechner, *Wishful Thinking: A Theological ABC* (New York Harper & Row, 1973), 95.

Chapter 15: Visionary

1. I am indebted to Joe McLamb for this insight.

2. A. W. Tozer, *The Best of A. W. Tozer,* compiled by Warren W. Wiersbe (Grand Rapids: Baker Book House, 1978), 49–52.

3. Quoted in Richard Higginson, *Transforming Leadership: A Christian Approach to Management* (London: SPCK, 1996), 84.

Chapter 16: Strategic

1. The strategy of strengthening churches will be considered in chapter 19: Communicative, and the strategy of developing leaders in chapter 17: Team-Building.

2. Bruce, *Paul,* 315.

3. "Fourth missionary journey" is presented this way because it is of quite a different character than the first three journeys.

4. How their companions Timothy and Luke escape the beating and imprisonment is not told.

5. John Pollock, *The Apostle: A Life of Paul* (New York: Doubleday, 1969), 157–58.

6. Meyer, *Paul,* 90.

7. Pollock, *The Apostle,* 173.

8. Pollock, *The Apostle,* 86.

Chapter 17: Team-Building

1. MacArthur, *Called to Lead,* 169.

2. Ascough and Cotton, *Passionate Visionary,* 82.

3. Ascough and Cotton, *Passionate Visionary,* 151–65.

4. Ascough and Cotton, *Passionate Visionary,* 153.

5. Dee Hock, *Birth of the Chaordic Age* (San Francisco: Berrett-Koehler, 1999). Cited in Ascough and Cotton, *Passionate Visionary,* 153–54.

6. Ascough and Cotton, *Passionate Visionary,* 111–13.

7. Paul's handling of conflict here is instructive. Dean Flemming observes that Paul also calls on someone else to mediate their conflict, involving the community in their reconciliation. Dean Flemming, *Philippians: A Commentary in the Wesleyan Tradition,* New Beacon Bible Commentary (Kansas City, MO: Beacon Hill Press of Kansas City, 2009), 213–18, 227–28.

8. For more on delegation, see Eddie Estep, *What's in Your Hand? Leadership Lessons from the Life of Moses* (Kansas City, MO: The Foundry Publishing, 2020), 120–27.

Chapter 19: Communicative

1. Sanders, *Paul the Leader*, 55.
2. Meyer, *Paul*, 124.
3. Bruce, *Paul*, 248.
4. Pollock, *The Apostle*, 167.
5. Meyer, *Paul*, 131.

Part 5: The Leader's Challenges

1. Personal correspondence between Joe McLamb and myself, July 22, 2022.
2. Tod Bolsinger, *Tempered Resilience: How Leaders are Formed in the Crucible of Change* (Downers Grove, IL: InterVarsity Press, 2020), 37.
3. Bolsinger, *Tempered Resilience*, 29.

Chapter 20: Criticism

1. Swindoll, *Paul*, 261–62.
2. For a treatment of how God uses Moses's inadequacy, see Estep, *What's in Your Hand?*, 67–71.
3. Swindoll, *Paul*, 263.
4. Swindoll, *Paul*, 263–70.

Chapter 21: Conflict

1. I am indebted to Michael Pitts for this insight.
2. Swindoll, *Paul*, 177–78.
3. Swindoll, *Paul*, 129.

Chapter 22: Crisis

1. Bruce, *Paul,* 351.
2. MacArthur, *Called to Lead*, 8.
3. It should be noted that Joshua Project estimates that evangelical Christians make up about 1.5 percent of the population. See https://joshuaproject.net/countries/MT.
4. Wright, Paul, 393.